Never miss a BBC Prom

All 84 BBC Proms concerts are
broadcast live on BBC Radio 3.

And you can listen again at your leisure
for up to seven days after broadcast
at bbc.co.uk/radio3.

BBC RADIO

90 — 93FM

THE PROMS 1895–2008

The Proms were founded to bring the best of classical music to a wide audience in an informal setting. From the very outset, part of the audience has always stood in the 'promenade'. Prom places originally cost just a shilling (5p); today, standing places at the Royal Albert Hall cost only £5.00, and over 1,000 tickets go on sale for every concert from an hour beforehand. Programmes have always mixed the great classics with what Henry Wood, the first conductor of the Proms, called his 'novelties' – in other words, rare works and premieres.

1895 The 26-year-old Henry Wood is chosen to launch the Promenade Concerts at the newly opened Queen's Hall, Langham Place; Wood conducts the Proms throughout their first 50 years 1927 The BBC takes over the running of the Proms 1930 The new BBC Symphony Orchestra becomes the orchestra of the Proms 1939 Proms season abandoned after only three weeks following the declaration of war 1941 The Proms move to the Royal Albert Hall after the Queen's Hall is gutted in an air raid 1942 The BBC Symphony Orchestra shares the season for the first time with another orchestra: the London Philharmonic 1947 First televised Last Night 1961 First complete opera heard at the Proms: Mozart's *Don Giovanni*, given by Glyndebourne Festival Opera 1966 First foreign orchestra at the Proms: the Moscow Radio Orchestra, under Gennady Rozhdestvensky 1970 First Late Night Prom: cult pop group The Soft Machine 1971 First 'world music' Prom: sitar-player Imrat Khan 1994 The Proms celebrate their 100th season with a retrospective of past premieres 1995 The Proms celebrate their centenary year with a season of new commissions 1996 First Proms Chamber Music series; first Prom in the Park 1998 First Blue Peter Family Prom signalling a new commitment to music for families 2002 The Proms go digital on BBC Four; on-demand listening begins online 2003 Proms in the Park reach out to all four nations of the UK with the unique festive atmosphere of the Last Night 2005 Proms Chamber Music moves to Cadogan Hall, the movies return to the Proms, and Henry Wood's *Fantasia on British Sea-Songs* celebrates its centenary 2008 Pre-Prom events – Proms Plus – expand to precede every main evening Proms concert.

THE BBC: bringing the Proms to you – in concert, on radio, television and online bbc.co.uk/proms

34
28
38
12
20
60
52
70

BBC PROMS

FSC Mixed Sources
Product group from well-managed forests, controlled sources and recycled wood or fiber
Cert no. SA-COC-1502
www.fsc.org
© 1996 Forest Stewardship Council

Cover illustration: Andy Potts. **This page:** Tony Russell/LWT/Boosey & Hawkes Collection/ArenaPal (Carter); Lebrecht Music & Arts (Rachmaninov); Clive Barda/ArenaPal (Stockhausen); Brian Seed/Lebrecht Music & Arts (Vaughan Williams); Shutterstock/Andy Potts/Private Collection/Roger-Viollet, Paris/Bridgeman Art Library (Messiaen); Chris Christodoulou (young audience, Last Night of the Proms); Shuttlestock (Proms Plus)

WELCOME TO THE BBC PROMS 2008

As **Roger Wright** takes up his new role as Director of the Proms, he introduces a new season packed with international artists and orchestras, a kaleidoscopic range of composer anniversaries and a sprinkling of unique festive touches. With a host of connections across more than 80 concerts, a new range of Proms Plus introductory events and a free afternoon Prom during the opening weekend – there's something to satisfy all tastes at the BBC Proms this summer

Andy Potts (po illustration); BBC (po Roger Wright); Chris Christodoulou (BBC SO); Malcolm Crowthers (Carter, Messiaen); photos.com (mixing desk)

A new role, a new challenge

It is a huge honour and pleasure for me to take over this unique institution and to guide the world's greatest music festival through the next chapter of its illustrious history.

A festival such as the Proms can only be made possible through great teamwork and partnerships. I am extremely fortunate to be able to work with exceptional colleagues in the BBC and also with so many friends and colleagues in the music industry, whose goodwill and spirit of collaboration have been inspiring.

I owe a huge debt of gratitude to my predecessors at the Proms – William Glock, Robert Ponsonby, John Drummond and Nicholas Kenyon – from whom I have learnt so much, both directly and indirectly; I have inherited from Nicholas a festival in rude health.

We have a truly unrivalled range of conductors, soloists and orchestras from around the world – just a flick through the listings will reveal appearances from Daniel Barenboim with his West-Eastern Divan Orchestra, Sir Simon Rattle with the Berliner Philharmoniker, Bernard Haitink with the Chicago Symphony Orchestra, and soloists such as Lang Lang, Janine Jansen and Sir John Tomlinson. But we are equally lucky to be able to call upon the five BBC orchestras and the BBC Singers and BBC choruses,

who collectively form the backbone of the festival. The management teams of these ensembles play a crucial role in the Proms planning process, and it's thrilling to be witnessing a period in which all the BBC performing groups are in such strong artistic form.

Continued innovation, inspired by the past

The Proms must continue to stimulate new ideas and offer innovative ways of presenting music. This year you'll see we're celebrating important anniversaries (including the centenaries of Elliott Carter and Olivier Messiaen), moving away from the thematic threads of recent years; and we are presenting a number of three-part programmes, as well as building on some historical programmes by repeating them – but with a contemporary twist.

The innovations of founder-conductor Henry Wood in juxtaposing the standard classics with contemporary and less familiar works remain vital to the Proms. As a tribute to him, in addition to the Proms premiere of Ethel Smyth's rare Concerto for Violin and Horn (dedicated to Wood), we are including two of Wood's magnificent orchestral transcriptions. This season you will also find some concerts on a massive scale that Wood himself would surely recognise!

The best orchestras from around the world | **Elliott Carter at 100** | **Messiaen centenary** | **Electroacoustic explorations**

Radio 3 New Generation Artists at the Proms

Aronowitz Ensemble	8 September, PCM 8
Sharon Bezaly *flute*	17 August, Prom 43
Allan Clayton *tenor*	11 August, Prom 34
Danjulo Ishizaka *cello*	19 August, Prom 45
Alexei Ogrintchouk *oboe*	19 August, Prom 45
Gwilym Simcock *composer/piano*	9 August, Prom 31
Elizabeth Watts *soprano*	8 September, PCM 8
	10 September, Prom 73

The Radio 3 NGA scheme is supported by Aviva plc

I hope too that the Late Night concerts will have a special atmosphere of their own, with everything from early choral Masses to Indian classical ragas. Electroacoustic music will feature too, and not only in the Late Night series.

I am delighted that, in this Vaughan Williams anniversary year, we have been able to programme a wide variety of British music – of which Henry Wood was such a champion. He gave the first performances of many British works – including, perhaps most famously, Vaughan Williams's *Serenade to Music*, which you can hear on the exact anniversary of the composer's death 50 years ago. This year's Proms will provide the chance not only to hear much of Vaughan Williams's music but also to place it in context – with works by his teachers, friends, fellow students and others influenced by him. In addition, Vaughan Williams's love of folk song finds a reflection in some other programmes, not least in Folk Day – a feature of our new-look opening weekend, which includes a free concert.

The spirit of '58, and other anniversaries

Looking through the programmes of previous Proms seasons makes for interesting reading. The year 1958 has a special significance and so we are reflecting some other elements from that notable year. The BBC Symphony Orchestra recreates a programme of Mendelssohn and Brahms from a Prom that year (although we have added an extra interval to suit modern trends!). In that season all five Rachmaninov piano concertos were performed, and so we are also recreating that mini-festival together with other Rachmaninov pieces this year. In a fascinating contrast, that same year saw the premiere, in Brussels, of Edgard Varèse's pioneering *Poème électronique* (see Prom 45) and of *Gruppen* by Karlheinz Stockhausen; this masterpiece for three orchestras is just one part of our Stockhausen Day on 2 August, and we are only sorry that the composer, who died last December, did not live to join us in his 80th-birthday year.

Other composers with significant anniversaries in 2008 include Simon Holt, Magnus Lindberg, Michael Berkeley, Nigel Osborne, Thea Musgrave, Einojuhani Rautavaara and Krzysztof Penderecki.

Vaughan Williams anniversary

Daniel Barenboim

Remembering Stockhausen

A folk fix from Kathryn Tickell

We are also celebrating the 40th birthday of two of our best-loved British ensembles – the King's Singers and the London Sinfonietta. The inaugural concert of the London Sinfonietta included *The Whale* by John Tavener, the work that helped establish the composer's reputation in the late 1960s; the narrator on that occasion was the BBC announcer Alvar Lidell, whose centenary falls this year – so it seemed natural to feature this remarkable work in one of the London Sinfonietta's two Proms this year.

More 'moments' for 2008

There is an increasing audience for opera in concert and we are delighted to be able to present three one-act operas (Janáček's *Osud*, Puccini's *Il tabarro* and Rimsky-Korsakov's *Kashchey the Immortal*). Other distinctive features this year include the Sunday-afternoon concerts in August, including four organ recitals; a number of leading artists giving more than one concert; a galaxy of young stars from Radio 3's New Generation Artists scheme (see box far left); and a gala concert featuring the winners of the 2008 Radio 3 Awards for World Music.

Across more than 80 concerts there are too many wonderful performers to mention. It is always a pleasure to bring familiar artists and ensembles back to the Proms but this year, after an absence of two decades, it is especially exciting to welcome Murray Perahia and Nigel Kennedy.

Of course, the Proms is about much more than the concerts. Throughout the festival there are talks, discussions, films, workshops, Composer Portrait concerts and a range of Proms Learning activities. For 2008, in a new venture at the Royal College of Music, there will be a fun and informative introductory event before every main evening Prom, and we are launching the Proms Literary Festival as part of this series of Proms Plus activities. Look out also for the family events and for the first ever Doctor Who Prom!

I offer my thanks to all those responsible for bringing the Proms to a wider audience through our broadcasts on radio, television and online. I grew up listening to the Proms on Radio 3 and they formed an essential part of my musical education. Not only is it the world's greatest music festival, but it can boast the most loyal, committed and enthusiastic of audiences. So, wherever you are, I hope you enjoy a marvellous summer at the BBC Proms 2008.

Roger Wright

Roger Wright
Controller, BBC Radio 3 and Director, BBC Proms

Awards for World Music   **Nigel Kennedy returns**   **A unique summer of music-making**   **Out of this world: the Doctor Who Prom**

'3 ISSUES FOR £1'

When you subscribe by Direct Debit to *BBC Music Magazine* today

BBC Music Magazine is your essential guide to the world of classical music. Every issue is full of the latest news, reviews and thought-provoking features. **PLUS** you'll receive an exclusive cover CD of complete works with every issue

GREAT REASONS TO SUBSCRIBE

- Your first 3 issues for just £1
- Continue to pay just £9.99 every 3 issues, saving 25% off the shop price
- **FREE CD** with every issue
- Every issue delivered direct to your door with **FREE** UK delivery
- Never miss an issue of the world's best selling classical music magazine

To take advantage of this fantastic offer simply:

Visit: **www.subscribeonline.co.uk/musicmagazine**

Or call us on: **0844 844 0252**

Calls to this number from a BT landline will cost no more than 5p per minute.
Calls from mobiles and other providers may vary.

PLEASE QUOTE MUPR08

SPECIAL INTRODUCTORY OFFER ● SPECIAL INTRODUCTORY OFFER ● SPECIAL INTRODUCTORY OFFER ● SPECIAL INTRODUCTORY OF

Free your iPod

Introducing the all new B&W Zeppelin: Forty years of leading the world of loudspeaker design now available at your nearest B&W stockist. Bring your iPod and experience the new B&W Zeppelin live-like sound or visit www.bowers-wilkins.com

Bowers & Wilkins

B&W makes the world's most advanced home theatre, hi-fi and iPod® speakers, used by music lovers everywhere. **Listen and you'll see.**

TWO-WAY VISION

VAUGHAN WILLIAMS (1872–1958)

Fifty years after the composer's death,
Stephen Johnson argues that Vaughan Williams's
reputation as a proponent of cosy English
pastoralism has obscured his willingness to take
an unblinkered look at the darker side of life

Anniversaries are rarely better timed than this one. No
20th-century British composer stands more in need of
reassessment than Ralph Vaughan Williams. You might
wonder why a composer who always seems to top the classical
charts should be a candidate for urgent revaluation. It's not as
though the work that regularly emerges as the nation's favourite,
The Lark Ascending, is anything less than top-drawer VW. But when
pieces such as this, or the equally familiar *Fantasia on 'Greensleeves'*,
are manipulated to sustain an image of the composer as – in the
words of *The Observer*'s Mary Riddell – 'the eulogist of Cream Tea
England', then a serious injustice is being done. More to the point,
it is proof that we have lost contact with the real core of Vaughan
Williams's vision – and, for once, that hideously overused word is
apt. Far from being a dreamy nostalgist, Vaughan Williams was a
true modern: a highly original musical thinker whose greatest works

bear the imprint of their times as much as those of Mahler and Shostakovich, and who has as much to say to us now as ever.

Let's start with *The Lark Ascending*, for solo violin and orchestra. Yes, on one level it is an exquisitely touching piece of musical birdwatching. What the poet George Meredith called the 'chirrup, whistle, slur and shake' of the skylark's song is captured with an ease and lifelike fluency that is somehow also perfectly attuned to the nature of the violin. At the same time it's a

We have lost contact with the real core of Vaughan Williams's vision – and, for once, that hideously overused word is apt.

triumphant fusion of observed birdsong with the rhythms and modal inflections of English folk music, which Vaughan Williams had devotedly collected, catalogued and studied with his friend and fellow-enthusiast Gustav Holst. But there's another, more unsettling dimension, most apparent at the ending, in which the violin-lark's song vanishes skywards, fading at last into an almost inaudible 'dying fall' of a minor third. In a good performance it can be almost unbearably poignant, as though the music were hovering on the brink of an abyss – which in a sense it is. Vaughan Williams composed *The Lark Ascending* in 1914, on the eve of the 'war to end all wars'. In his heart he surely realised that the dream of an English pastoral Eden was as doomed as the young men who worked the land and sang its ancient songs. Like Holst's exactly contemporary 'Mars' from *The Planets*, *The Lark Ascending* confronts the coming horror, but much more subtly, and with far greater poignancy.

This uncomfortable dual-sidedness is typical of so many of Vaughan Williams's finest works. Take another old favourite, the *Fantasia on a Theme by Thomas Tallis*. Here we find more pastoral folk colouring, a string orchestra set out in discrete 'choirs' evoking the misty spaces of Gloucester Cathedral (for which it was written), and Tallis's Elizabethan hymn at the core adding a suitable Olde English flavour – or so it seems. In fact the exploitation of space as an element of musical drama is strikingly modern – Sir Harrison Birtwistle, no less, acknowledges it as a formative musical influence. The use of modal harmonies and free-floating, quasi-improvisatory

folk rhythms is unlike anything in British music before (this is 1910): the rhythmic 'contraction' at the climax (3/4–5/8–4/8–3/8) is as daring and innovatory as anything the continental modernists were coming up with at the time. At the same time Vaughan Williams hints at much darker meanings: a reference to the death-intoxicated cantata *Toward the Unknown Region* in the ethereal opening chords ties up eerily with the words VW set to Tallis's hymn in his then-controversial *English Hymnal*: 'When rising from my bed of death'. The glorious wide-spaced string chord at the start (in itself a brilliant piece of scoring) hovers for a moment like a memory of something primal and pure, then fades for ever. As a whole the *Tallis Fantasia* can be understood as an increasingly impassioned quest to recapture that fleeting vision – a quest that fails.

Here we catch more than a glimpse of the artist whom a friend memorably summed up as 'the Christian Agnostic'. Vaughan Williams was drawn again and again to religious subjects – the Anglican liturgy, the Latin Mass, the Bible, John Bunyan's *Pilgrim's Progress*, William Blake's idiosyncratic reinterpretation of the Book of Job – but he could also immerse himself in Walt Whitman's pantheistic transcendentalism in his *Sea Symphony* or in Shakespeare's nihilistic Prospero speech, 'We are such stuff as dreams are made on' in his little choral masterpiece *Three Shakespeare Songs*. With Whitman he could sing 'Bathe me, O God, in thee' with spine-tingling fervour; and yet one suspects that there ▶

ABOVE
The fan-vaulted lavatorium of Gloucester Cathedral. Vaughan Williams's *Tallis Fantasia* was premiered in the building in 1910

BELOW LEFT
'The Lord answering Job out of the Whirlwind': the 13th of William Blake's 21 illustrations for the Book of Job, the inspiration for Vaughan Williams's 'masque for dancing'

Music flourishing at Charterhouse in 2008

Ralph Vaughan Williams at Charterhouse in 1888

Whatever Vaughan Williams may have said to the contrary, the Sixth Symphony bears the imprint of the recently concluded Second World War like an open wound.

Sixth all is harshness, turbulence, dissonance. Whatever Vaughan Williams may have said to the contrary, this symphony bears the imprint of the recently concluded Second World War like an open wound: the inhuman repeated trumpet-and-drum rhythm in the second movement; the Scherzo's saxophone paying bitter tribute to a jazz musician killed in a Luftwaffe bombing raid. But ultimately VW was right: this is not a 'War Symphony'. The extraordinary Epilogue looks deeper than that. *Pianissimo* (very quiet, and virtually expressionless) throughout, it unfolds – if that's the word – in almost aimless drifting. Scraps of themes gradually home in on two chords: a sigh, or an 'Amen', that remains hopelessly impaled on its own dissonance – a dissonance that isn't even resolved at the very end. This from the composer of 'For all the saints' and 'Come down, O Love divine': two of the most uplifting hymns in the Anglican hymnbook. Vaughan Williams is said to have been delighted when the composer Rutland Boughton described this unique anti-finale as 'the Agnostic's Paradisum'. It seems the very antithesis of the image of faith so movingly created at the close of the Fifth Symphony, as bleak and comfortless in its own way as anything by Shostakovich.

Vaughan Williams's ability to balance these two antithetical visions – the Christian and the Agnostic, transcendent aspiration and realistic despair – without seeking a false, dubiously consoling synthesis, is the true mark of his greatness. That, and his unflagging ability to find the right musical means with which to express it. His last major work, the Ninth Symphony (completed at the age of 85), ends with a breathtaking distillation of this paradox. In the midst of a gaunt, slab-like orchestral landscape a dazzling chord of E major cuts through like an impossible sunburst. But, as it rises and ▶

was a part of him that might equally have enjoyed Richard Dawkins's *The God Delusion*. This is not a mark of intellectual or spiritual confusion, rather a sign of courageous honesty. Like Jung or William James, Vaughan Williams knew there was *something* in religious experience, even if it eluded the formulations of any credo. He explored what it meant to him in his operatic 'morality' *The Pilgrim's Progress*, and still more movingly and originally in his wonderful Fifth Symphony, which reworks themes from the opera in a beautifully spun symphonic drama, finally resolving tension in a serene recreation of the sound of Tudor church music.

But Vaughan Williams also knew that, in the words of Thomas Hardy, 'If a way to the better there be, it entails a full look at the worst'. The journey and final outcome of the Sixth Symphony (1944–7) could hardly be further from the Fifth's warm benediction. Like the Fifth, the Symphony No. 6 begins with a kind of musical question: 'What key am I in?' But where in No. 5 the ambiguity is relatively mild, the scoring soft and romantically beguiling, in the

LEFT
Vaughan Williams conducting the premiere of his Fifth Symphony, at the Proms in 1943

BELOW
Henry Wood, founder-conductor of the Proms, with the original 16 soloists for Vaughan Williams's *Serenade to Music*. Written specially for Wood's Jubilee Concert on 5 October 1938, the piece is said to have reduced Rachmaninov (who performed in the same concert, see page 35) to tears

BBC (above & below right)

EDINBURGH INTERNATIONAL
FESTIVAL 08

8-31 AUGUST

ACCEPT NO BORDERS

KURT WEILL CITY OF MAHAGONNY **SUSAN BICKLEY** SIR WILLARD WHITE
HK GRUBER ROYAL SCOTTISH NATIONAL ORCHESTRA **DMITRI HVOROSTOVSKY**
YSAŸE QUARTET **SCOTTISH OPERA** SMETANA THE TWO WIDOWS **BBCSSO**
MESSIAEN **ESTONIAN PHILHARMONIC CHAMBER CHOIR** PAUL MEYER
NAJI HAKIM ITRI **GOTHENBURG SYMPHONY ORCHESTRA** GUSTAVO DUDAMEL
SISTER MARIE KEYROUZ SCOTTISH CHAMBER ORCHESTRA **ISRAEL IN EGYPT**
CHANT WARS **FINNISH RADIO SYMPHONY ORCHESTRA KARITA MATTILA**
KEITH LEWIS **MELVYN TAN** A CUMPAGNIA **VALERY GERGIEV** LONDON SYMPHONY
ORCHESTRA **PROKOFIEV SYMPHONIES** BELCEA QUARTET **ANCHISKHATI**
STEVE REICH **LEONIDAS KAVAKOS** ORCHESTRE REVOLUTIONNAIRE ET ROMANTIQUE
SIR JOHN ELIOT GARDINER MONTEVERDI CHOIR **SUSAN BULLOCK** STEPHANE DENEVE
SIR CHARLES MACKERRAS FAZIL SAY **ALFRED BRENDEL** MISCHA MAISKY
LES ARTS FLORISSANTS PAVEL HAAS QUARTET **BUDAPEST FESTIVAL ORCHESTRA**
IVAN FISCHER **CHRISTINE SCHÄFER** SZYMANOWSKI KING ROGER **MARIINSKY OPERA**
IRVINE ARDITTI **COLLEGIUM VOCALE GENT** PHILIPPE HERREWEGHE **KATARINA KARNEUS**
STAATSKAPELLE DRESDEN **FABIO LUISI** IVAN MORAVEC **HEINER GOEBBELS**
JERUSALEM QUARTET **TIPPETT A CHILD OF OUR TIME** BEAUX ARTS TRIO
BANK OF SCOTLAND FIREWORKS CONCERT

**FREE BROCHURE
0131 473 2000
eif.co.uk**

falls in huge waves, the chord is blurred by dissonant harmonies on three saxophones. It recalls the elderly W. B. Yeats, crying out similarly in the face of death: 'Shall we in that great night rejoice?' The radiant E major chord affirms, the saxophones sound rather less convinced. We are left with two possibilities, and challenged to make our own way between them.

Yet perhaps there is a kind of answer. Not long after Vaughan Williams completed his convulsively violent, modernist Fourth Symphony (1931–4) and his choral-orchestral prayer for peace, *Dona nobis pacem* (1936), he turned again to Shakespeare in one of his warmest, most delicious works, the *Serenade to Music* (1938).

> Vaughan Williams's ability to balance the antithetical visions of the Christian and the Agnostic is the true mark of his greatness.

This sets words from the final scene of *The Merchant of Venice*, in which music is portrayed as offering a possibility of reconciliation and transcendence that the play's ostensible Christian morality so strikingly fails to provide. And here, surely, is a key. The composer who helped set up the National Youth Orchestra, who offered his support to young composers through the Society for the Promotion of New Music, who championed folk music as a living resource rather than as 'heritage', and galvanised this country's amateur choral societies into a powerful social force in wartime, seems to have known ultimately where hope still lay. Perhaps that's why even his bleakest music – the Epilogue of the Sixth Symphony, the coldly inhuman 'Landscape' movement of the *Sinfonia antartica* (1949–52) – is never really depressing. Samuel Beckett, often portrayed as theatre's great nihilist, candidly admitted that the urge to express in itself contradicted the seeming despair at the heart of works like *Waiting for Godot* and *Krapp's Last Tape*: 'If I really believe in nothing, why bother to say so?' If saying something expresses hope, how much more so does singing about it? In an age when culture seems to offer distraction rather than anything genuinely affirmative, it is a message we need to hear. ●

Stephen Johnson has written regularly for The Independent, The Guardian *and* BBC Music Magazine, *and is the author of books on Bruckner, Mahler and Wagner. He is a regular presenter of BBC Radio 3's* Discovering Music.

VAUGHAN WILLIAMS AT THE PROMS

24 July, Prom 10	Symphony No. 4
29 July, Prom 16	Symphony No. 8
8 August, Prom 29	Five Variants of 'Dives and Lazarus'; Symphony No. 6
12 August, Prom 35	Piano Concerto
17 August, Prom 43	Flos campi
26 August, Prom 54	Fantasia on a Theme by Thomas Tallis; Job: A Masque for Dancing; Serenade to Music; Symphony No. 9
27 August, Prom 55	The Lark Ascending
1 September, PCM 7	On Wenlock Edge
10 September, Prom 73	Sinfonia antartica (Symphony No. 7)
13 September, Prom 76	Sea Songs

BBC Symphony Orchestra

Jiří Bělohlávek Chief Conductor

The BBC Symphony Orchestra at the Barbican
October 2008 – May 2009

The Barbican's Associate Orchestra

LANDMARK EVENTS

Elliott Carter Centenary Concert

Three Composer Days focusing on the music of Stockhausen, Tristan Murail and Xenakis

Falla's *El amor brujo* **(Love, the Magician)** featuring flamenco singer Montse Cortés

Julietta Jiří Bělohlávek conducts Martinů's surrealist opera

Tan Dun *The Map: Concerto for Cello, Video and Orchestra*

GREAT ORCHESTRAL WORKS

Great symphonies from Bruckner, Dvořák and Tchaikovsky

Strauss *Ein Heldenleben*

Violin concertos by Ligeti, Mozart and Stravinsky with Gil Shaham and Alina Ibragimova

Haydn Cello Concertos

VOCAL AND CHORAL MASTERPIECES

Beethoven *Missa solemnis*

Bruckner *Mass No. 3 in F minor*

Orff *Carmina burana*

Poulenc *Stabat Mater*

With the BBC Symphony Chorus and soloists including Christine Brewer, Karen Cargill, Annick Massis, Sally Matthews, William Dazeley and Paul Groves

Mahler *Lieder eines fahrenden Gesellen* with Dagmar Pecková

Strauss *Drei Hymnen* with Soile Isokoski

OUTSTANDING NEW MUSIC

Premieres of works by Benet Casablancas, Guillaume Connesson, Brian Elias, Sam Hayden, Svatopluk Havelka, Vic Hoyland, Magnus Lindberg, Matthias Pintscher, Jukka Tiensuu

barbican

Box Office
020 7638 8891 (bkg fee)
www.barbican.org.uk
Reduced booking fee online

Visit bbc.co.uk/symphonyorchestra for full details of all concerts and to sign up for the BBC SO e-newsletter

BBC RADIO 3

90 – 93FM

THE LIGHT OF SOUND

OLIVIER MESSIAEN (1908–92)

In the centenary year of the composer's birth, **Paul Griffiths** offers 100 reminiscences of a visionary musician who understood his art as coloured time

Born 100 years ago, Olivier Messiaen wrote some of the 20th century's most astonishing music. He was a devout Catholic and, in a godless age, went on illuminating the triumphs of his faith – in orchestral works, songs, organ and piano music, an oratorio, and an opera on the life and death of St Francis.

But Messiaen's religion was also, and perhaps primarily, a religion of sound, a glorying in rich harmony, rhythmic fascination and excitement, soaring melody and bursts of wild exuberance modelled on birdsong. Remembering him now, the man and his music, what comes to mind is a rush of moments and fragments ...

A critic for over 30 years, including for *The Times* and *The New Yorker*, Paul Griffiths is an authority on 20th- and 21st-century music. Among his books are studies of Boulez, Cage, Messiaen and Stravinsky, as well as the recent *A Concise History of Western Music*; he also writes novels and librettos.

the language of love in the *Turangalîla Symphony*,
as familiar as if in a film score

the unearthly strangeness, too: *that paradox*

ticking clocks and triumphant rapture
bounding through 10 movements   the brimming passion in the exotic-
erotic song-cycle *Harawi*

the chimes of love again in the choral *Cinq rechants*

how he created something unique here: how he would sit in his aisle seat during
a triptych of three unalike parts   intervals, the many times he came to London,
calmly signing programmes for admirers

how his music goes on clamouring
in the mind and will not finish   the ethereal swooping in *Turangalîla* of the
electronic ondes martenot, like a non-human
voice, the voice of an angel

the sound there, too, of glittering piano virtuosity

the sheer thrill of the orchestra   the imitation of natural sounds: wind through
sedges, wind in high places, waterfalls

the unmistakably personal
sound of every bar   the impersonality of music that speaks
with its own voice: *that paradox*

the grandeur of *La Transfiguration* at the First Night
of the Proms, 38 years ago   the mountain setting of this
piece and the mountain music

birds as similar, daily miracles

'A passion for symmetry'
Jennifer Bate *organist*

When recording Messiaen's *Livre du Saint Sacrement* together at La Trinité, we finished ahead of schedule. Messiaen invited me to spend our free day at his home. During the visit he suddenly asked me whether I would like to see where he composed. Unlocking another apartment in the building, he said that, until then, only his wife had ever seen this room.

Everything inside was meticulously ordered, revealing his passion for symmetry. On the table was a draughtsman's board with a vast orchestral score under preparation. Across the base was a collection of pencils, each sharpened to perfection, forming a perfect triangle. Nearby lay a pyramid of books, also arranged by size with great precision. On the wall stood a frame consisting of three rows of three compartments, each containing exquisite wood carvings of Nativity figures. He told me that he had contemplated these each day while writing *La Nativité du Seigneur*.

the imitation above all of the calls
and songs of birds   the shrieks that announce the
angel in the opera *Saint Francis of Assisi*

how he sat at interview – serene, yet attentive   the sense of space, of cathedral vaults, of mountain-tops

also the brilliant mountain light   also the revelation of divinity
on earth, Jesus seen by his disciples
transfigured

birds as winged like angels, flying
like the resurrected

birds as shimmering with the colours of paradise   birds as bearers of divine music,
untaught and uncomposed

'Come back, come back!'
Pierre-Laurent Aimard *pianist and conductor*

In the summer of 1987 – at the Centre Acanthes in Avignon, where Messiaen was a special guest – I performed in the *Turangalîla Symphony* outdoors, by the Palais des Papes. As soon as we began, menacing clouds gathered. The wind became violent, the musical scores blew away, the air became saturated with humidity. Suddenly, a downpour fell on the crowd and the stage. The audience rushed to the narrow exits; members of the orchestra took flight, protecting their instruments as best they could.

In the first row of the terraced seats, sheltered under a gigantic, hastily deployed umbrella, Messiaen (who seemed not to have realised what was going on, since he was lost in following the score) stood up, indignant, and, raising his finger, cried to the orchestra: 'But what are you doing? Come back, come back, I order you to continue!'

how from the organ he could unleash blazing mystery into
a wintry church, no matter how diminished the congregation   his invisibility in the organ loft

his devotion in serving as organist
at La Trinité in Paris for over six decades   the devotion of his listeners and performers
– atheist, Jewish, Buddhist: *that paradox*

how nothing human – no person,
no culture – was alien to him   how his religion marked a centre, not a boundary

how the organ was his first tutor in
orchestration, as he transferred *L'Ascension* from
ranks of pipes to families of instruments   the separate families in all his orchestral
scores, across the 60 years from *Les offrandes
oubliées* to the *Concert à quatre*

also the increasing subtlety of instrumental mixtures

the increasing dazzle, too, of tuned percussion

Bloomsbury Terrace
Huntley Street, WC1

A fabulous collection of luxury two bedroom apartments boasting stylish, contemporary interiors and traditional Edwardian architecture, set within the vibrant neighbourhood of bohemian Bloomsbury. Just minutes from the finest restaurants, shops and leafy squares, this desirable address enjoys the rich culture, colourful entertainment and artistic lifestyle of the West End.

Prices from **£699,995**

Tel: **0845 871 0095**

www.barratthomes.co.uk/bloomsburyterrace

♪♪ ALLOW US TO ORCHESTRATE YOUR NEXT MOVE ♪♪

Parkside,
Wandsworth SW18

Live alongside the park, enjoy great views and have everything within reach. Trains to Waterloo take just 17 minutes, or cross the River Thames to explore Chelsea and Fulham including the world famous Kings Road. Every contemporary 2 bedroom apartment in this striking building features full height glazing, creating light and space within this new landmark building.

Marketing Centre open daily 10.00am to 6.00pm

Prices from **£399,995**

Tel: **0845 871 0025**

www.wandsworthparkside.co.uk

BARRATT
HOMES

built around you

Details and prices are correct at time of going to press. All distances are approximate. Train times obtained from National Rail enquiries. Computer Generated Impressions.

'Warmth … encouragement'

George Benjamin *composer and conductor*

I was taken to meet Messiaen in April 1976, when I was just 16. He responded with surprising warmth to the naive pieces I played, and immediately invited me to become his student at the Paris Conservatoire. The class was famous internationally – his pupils had included Pierre Boulez, Karlheinz Stockhausen, Iannis Xenakis, Alexander Goehr, Tristan Murail and Gérard Grisey among many others. Messiaen would analyse Classical and modern works, including his own, in great detail. His views on harmony and rhythm were revelatory, and topics ranged from birdsong and non-Western music to plainchant and avant-garde instrumental techniques.

His encouragement to me was inspiring, and he engaged with students with exceptional attention and subtlety, aiming to serve them in the most humble way. These attributes – added to his remarkable capacity to encourage independent thought – still fill me with wonder.

how the light caught in his candy-floss white hair

the light that shines from and within his music

the source of that light in imitating natural resonance

how birds – nature's musicians – were his second, third and last tutors in orchestration

how birds of many instrumental lustres sing around the saint in *Saint Francis*

the voluble runs of the garden warbler, a favourite

the sense of music older than humanity – as light, resonance, colour and birdsong all are

the sense simultaneously of music never before imagined or imaginable: *that paradox*

the resounding of ancient traditions

the Indonesian percussion music that is not so much adopted or adapted as paralleled in *Turangalîla* and *La Transfiguration*

how he sat with his hands in his lap and spoke softly, his lips barely parting and always returning to that smile

the plainsong reborn in *La Transfiguration* and *Saint Francis*

the presence – again a parallel – of archaic ceremony in *Saint Francis*

the scales of his own devising that would turn anything – jazz, birdsong, Peruvian folk music – into Messiaen

into the space-filling power of his organ music – *Apparition de l'église éternelle*

into its exhilarating dynamism – *Joie et clarté des corps glorieux*

into its moments, too, of quieter meditation – in the *Messe de la Pentecôte, La Nativité du Seigneur* or any of the cycles he developed from his Sunday improvisations

the symmetrical rhythms circling through time

the repetitive patterns offering glimpses of changelessness

the representation of eternity also in extreme slowness – the two adagios of the *Quartet for the End of Time*

how he would happily discourse on his methods

how his many pupils learnt only to be themselves: *that paradox*

(Stockhausen becoming Stockhausen to create *Punkte*; a generation later, Benjamin becoming Benjamin to write *Ringed by the Flat Horizon*)

as if all his instruction were not in composition but listening

just as his music encourages us to listen

so that what we hear is, for example birdsong as never before

birdsong as heard by someone listening up close, everywhere

music made for the ear of God

music acknowledging darkness but infused mostly by glory

music moving towards glory, as in the final sections of *La Transfiguration* and *Saint Francis*.

how he sat quite still when playing the piano

the movement, the propulsion, all in the sound

and that stillness, also

as if he were innocent of the music

'A very special experience'

Myung-Whun Chung *conductor*

After becoming Music Director of the Opéra Bastille in 1989, I played the *Quartet for the End of Time* for the first time with musicians from the orchestra. Messiaen came to see us after the concert, and said: 'It's the most fabulous interpretation I've heard in my life' – moreover he wrote as much in my score. It was a very special experience. I later realised that he would say the same thing to other performers of his works at the end of their concerts. But what is more extraordinary is that he was entirely sincere and enthusiastic each time!

THSH

0121 780 3333
www.thsh.co.uk

TOWN HALL BIRMINGHAM   **SYMPHONY HALL** BIRMINGHAM

DISCOVER GREAT
PERFORMANCES
AT THE HEART OF BIRMINGHAM

TOWN HALL AND SYMPHONY HALL

Birmingham International
Concert Season now on sale

TOWN HALL RENOVATION FUNDED BY:

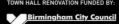

Heritage
LOTTERY FUNDED

PROJECT PART-FINANCED
BY THE EUROPEAN UNION
European Regional
Development Fund

music always in segments, extraordinarily different –
a majestic chorale, a clattering toccata, odd things
caught in the same time-frame   music compellingly whole: *that paradox*

the wholeness of heaven

the partial view from on earth   the wholeness of eternity

the stammering of time   how he would wear a brightly patterned shirt,
                                              open at the neck, under his sober jacket

the colours with which he would describe his music

'a wheeling, a gyrating interpenetration of superhuman
colours – these swords of fire, these blue and orange
lava flows', as he said of the *Quartet*

the image there too of the rainbow,
of the mighty angel of the Apocalypse,   the blue of tranquil A major,
'having a rainbow on his head'   of the sea, of the celestial

the jumble of colours tending to blue,   story-telling and pattern-making, as
as in medieval stained-glass   in the windows of Chartres Cathedral

the majestic blocks of *Et exspecto resurrectionem
mortuorum*, first heard with coloured light streaming
through the similar windows of the Sainte Chapelle,   a French Catholic organist-composer
much to the composer's contentment

one who learnt from Indian rhythmic
theory, Japanese court music, Peruvian   how he seemed lightly tethered
folk song: *that paradox*   to an immense confidence

how he travelled the world for his music and his birds'

evenings in concert halls,
mornings in fields and woods

MESSIAEN AT THE PROMS

18 July, Prom 1	La Nativité du Seigneur – Dieu parmi nous
21 July, PCM 1	Catalogue d'oiseaux – L'alouette lulu
21 July, Prom 6	L'Ascension (for organ); Et exspecto resurrectionem mortuorum
27 July, Prom 14	La Transfiguration de Notre Seigneur Jésus-Christ
3 August, Prom 22	Verset pour la Fête de la Dédicace; Prélude
6 August, Prom 27	L'Ascension (for orchestra)
10 August, Prom 32	Messe de la Pentecôte
11 August, PCM 4	Harawi
17 August, Prom 42	Apparition de l'église éternelle; La Nativité du Seigneur
19 August, Prom 45	Concert à quatre
1 September, Prom 63	Cinq rechants
2 September, Prom 64	Turangalîla Symphony
4 September, Prom 67	Quartet for the End of Time
7 September, Prom 70	Saint Francis of Assisi

'Absolutely captivated'

Yvonne Loriod *pianist, Messiaen's widow*

How did I first meet Messiaen? This was after he'd returned from being a prisoner of war … I was sent to join his class in harmony. At the class the pupils were absolutely astonished, because here was a man who was quite young and whose fingers were swollen on account of the privations which he suffered during his time in captivity in Silesia. He brought out the miniature score of Debussy's *Prélude à L'après-midi d'un faune*, placed it on the piano and played it to us … There he was, playing the piano with such beautiful sounds in spite of the deformity of his hands. We were absolutely captivated; the whole class adored him straight away.
From 'The Messiaen Companion', ed. Peter Hill, Faber & Faber Ltd

evenings in London – *Saint Francis*   mornings caught by the camera,
on his 80th birthday   notebook in hand, a beret on his head

always with his wife, the pianist Yvonne Loriod   their life going on in quiet – except
                                                                                    for Loriod's formidable playing

other things earlier – the prisoner-of-war camp
where the *Quartet* was composed   now the regular life of work   and the life beyond

how steady his gaze   how he left with one score, *Concert à quatre*,
                                            perhaps to finish later

what complexities he devised

how simple it all was: *that paradox*

Malcolm Crowthers

NORWAY

The first time you see the fjords is a moment you will never forget.

VISIT NORWAY .CO.UK

Let us take you on a journey of the senses. Crystal clear fjords, majestic mountains, uncrowded countryside and white sandy beaches – and it's a lot closer than you think. You'll discover breathtaking scenery, fresh mountain air and a vibrant culture, all designed to make you feel alive. Whether you take a coastal cruise or a short break, you'll never be far from nature at its most magnificent and unspoilt.

See, hear, smell, taste, touch Norway.

For your free Visit Norway pack **visitnorway.co.uk** or call **01443 828 818** quoting BBC01

NORWAY
POWERED BY NATURE

 www.visitnorway.co.uk

The Royal College of Music is delighted to be a part of this year's BBC Proms. Every day of the season you can enjoy Proms Plus in the College's exquisite 400-seat theatre, just across the road from the Royal Albert Hall.

When the BBC Proms are over, the music continues at the RCM. With over 200 annual concerts, acclaimed operas, free lectures, masterclasses, and a fascinating Museum of Instruments, the Royal College of Music is a great place to explore classical music and discover the most exciting young international talent.

For details of all upcoming performances, including our 125th anniversary series at Cadogan Hall, visit www.rcm.ac.uk.

"Superlative additions to London's musical life"
THE TIMES on Royal College of Music concerts

Royal College of Music

Prince Consort Road, London SW7 2BS
Box Office: 020 7591 4314 | Email info@rcm.ac.uk

RCM
LONDON

COMMUNING WITH THE COSMOS

KARLHEINZ STOCKHAUSEN (1928–2007)

Even before his death last year, this bright star among the 20th century's musical iconoclasts had been accused of losing his glow. **Tom Service** argues that the passage of time might shed a different light

'What I achieved in the last half-century is more than has been achieved in the last 700 years of musical history.' Karlheinz Stockhausen was not prone to understatement. His death in December last year, at the age of 79, marked the end of an era. For so many people, from cutting-edge electronica artists to avant-garde cognoscenti, from musicians such as Björk and Brian Eno to Helmut Lachenmann, Stockhausen was the guiding figure and inspiration of contemporary music. That he meant so many things to so many different musicians is a measure of the sheer range of his accomplishments. Whether or not you believe, as he did, that his achievements have dwarfed those of the rest of musical history, it's hard to think of any other composer who has influenced so much of the entirety of musical experience in the 20th and 21st centuries. From his pioneering, visionary work in the studios of the North-West German Radio in Cologne –

one of whose greatest products, *Kontakte* ('Contacts') for piano, percussion and electronics, you can hear as part of Stockhausen Day on 2 August – to the hallucinatory brilliance of *Stimmung* ('Tuning') for six voices, which will bring its shimmering radiance to the Late Night Prom the same day, not to mention the sheer scale and ambition of his *Licht* ('Light') cycle of seven operas, Stockhausen's music is the most wildly ambitious of any postwar composer.

But he was a composer who courted controversy as much as he inspired admiration, even adulation, in his students and his fans. In fact, it's easy to caricature him, especially in his later decades, as a combination of spiritual *naïf* and vainly arrogant egocentric. This, after all, was the man who claimed he came not from Earth, but from the star Sirius, and whose domestic arrangements were nothing if not eccentric (after two marriages and six children, he lived for the last decades of his life with two of his favourite instrumentalists, the flautist Kathinka Pasveer and clarinettist Suzanne Stephens). He thought nothing of sacrificing relationships with his children if they got in the way of his all-encompassing creativity, he infamously referred to the 9/11 attacks on New York as 'the greatest work of art ever' (a statement he qualified by saying this was an art-work 'by Lucifer'), and he wrote a string quartet in which each of the four musicians plays inside their own airborne helicopter. And the demands he placed on performers and institutions were nothing short of torturous: asking, for instance, that musicians starve themselves for a few days before attempting to perform his 1968 'intuitive music' *Aus den Sieben Tagen* ('From the Seven Days'). All that, and he was featured on the cover of the Beatles' *Sgt Pepper's Lonely Hearts Club Band*.

Since his death some people who knew him best have characterised his musical journey as a trajectory from the iconoclasm of the 1950s and 1960s to a self-obsessed spirituality, embodied above all by the mythology of the seven operas of *Light*, one for each day of the week. Pierre Boulez told me, when I talked to him for Radio 3's *Music Matters* just after Stockhausen's death, that he hadn't been able to have a meaningful conversation with Karlheinz for over 30 years, and this despite the fact that they were the twin figureheads of postwar music. Instead of the impassioned debates Stockhausen inspired at the Darmstadt summer schools in the early 1950s, he became a person who could not countenance any disagreement with his vision: there was his way, or the wrong way.

The inscrutable world of *Light*, on which he began work in the mid-1970s, is where many Stockhausen followers lose their faith in his work. How do you square the coruscating experimentation of a work like *Gruppen* (literally, 'Groups': it's scored for three orchestras) with the rambling narrative and sub-*Star Trek* costumes of, say, *Friday from Light*? And yet to dismiss his later music as mere wilful eccentricity is clearly to do it a huge

ABOVE
Three's company: Stockhausen in 1996 with clarinettist Suzanne Stephens (left) and flautist Kathinka Pasveer (right), the instrumentalists with whom he latterly lived

BELOW LEFT
Bright young things: at a rehearsal with fellow avant-gardists Pierre Boulez (left) and Bruno Maderna (middle), late 1950s

It's hard to think of any other composer who has influenced so much of the entirety of musical experience in the 20th and 21st centuries.

disservice. The fact is, we don't know what *Light* is really like. Until the whole thing is staged (there are plans for the first complete performances in Germany in 2010), no-one can actually put a finger on the true significance of this baffling cornucopia of ritualistic drama and instrumental theatre.

However, we can begin to put the record straight. It's not the case that there are two Stockhausens: a musical genius in his early compositional life who atrophied into a self-mythologising weirdo. After all, he was the same person, and there are close musical connections between everything Stockhausen wrote. The world ▶

of the terse, early *Klavierstücke* ('Piano Pieces') seems cosmically distant from the scale and sound-world of *Light* – or, for that matter, the unfinished *Klang* ('Sound') cycle he was working on at the end of his life (he completed 21 of the projected 24 hours of this work, and you can hear the world premiere of *Harmonien* for trumpet, part of the fifth hour of *Klang*, during Stockhausen Day, as well as *Cosmic Pulses*, the 13th hour). But they're closely related, both on a technical and poetic level. Stockhausen's musical revelations in the 1950s were twofold. Firstly, by investigating a world of total serialism (using predetermined sequences for pitch, rhythm, loudness), he insisted on a rigorous generating principle behind all of his musical material; and secondly, he created a new kind of musical

Pierre Boulez told me that he hadn't been able to have a meaningful conversation with Karlheinz for over 30 years.

time, a 'moment-form' that finds one of its key expressions in *Punkte* ('Points'), which you can hear on 22 August, the day that would have been his 80th birthday. Similarly, the *Light* cycle is a radical exploration of musical time and space. Time is expanded into newer and vaster dimensions, but the music is generated from a single musical idea, a 'superformula' from which the world of each opera evolves. The sound-world may be new, but the approach is similar to those works of the 1950s, in creating a quasi-serial musical gene that contains the blueprint of the whole work. There's something profoundly Teutonic, even Romantic, about all

this musical organicism used in the expression of a universalised spirituality. Stockhausen's biographer, Robin Maconie, sees Stockhausen precisely in a German mystical tradition, hearing his final works as a series of meditations on death and departure: works like the literally ethereal *Helicopter Quartet* or *Heaven's Door*, the fourth hour of the *Klang* cycle.

Our problem is trying to square the apparently revolutionary energy of the early music with the new worlds opened up by the later music. That's why some people have the issues they do with the man and the music. But I think these are our problems, not his. In fact, from the start, Stockhausen saw his music as a spiritual journey, something that's as true of the *Klavierstücke* as of the *Klang* cycle. We're now living in a post-Stockhausen world, and the weird paradox that befalls creative artists is beginning to emerge – where it's only once they're dead that we start to make sense of their whole output. I think that, as time goes on, we'll be hearing more connections, compositional and cosmic, across the whole range of Stockhausen's music. And the Proms couldn't be a better place to start. ●

Chief Music Critic of the *Guardian*, Tom Service contributes to numerous magazines and journals. Since 2003 he has presented *Music Matters*, Radio 3's topical weekly magazine programme.

STOCKHAUSEN AT THE PROMS

2 August, Prom 20	Gruppen; Cosmic Pulses; Harmonien; Kontakte; Gruppen
2 August, Prom 21	Stimmung
22 August, Prom 48	Punkte (1952/1962/1993)

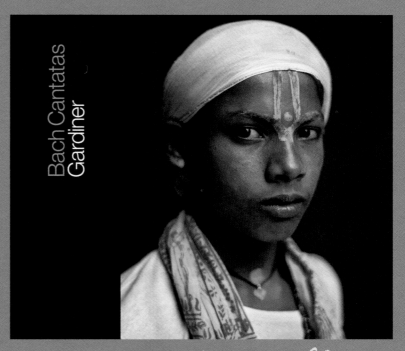

Soli Deo Gloria

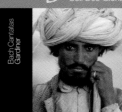

www.monteverdiproductions.co.uk or 020 7093 3984

A NEW ENCOUNTER

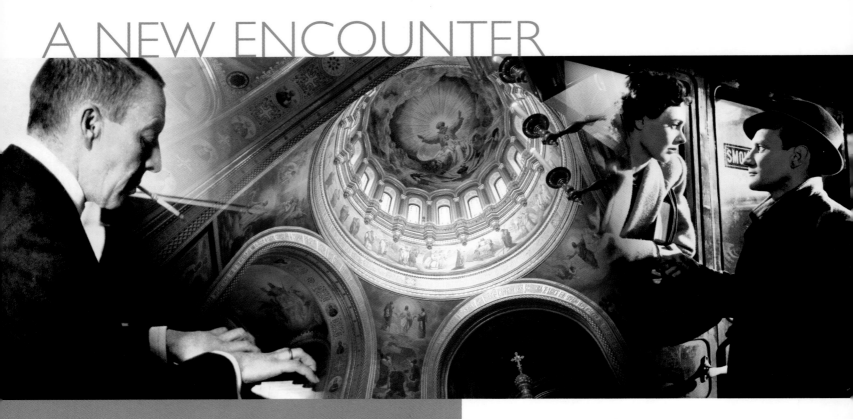

SERGEY RACHMANINOV (1873–1943)

A Proms season unusually rich in works by Rachmaninov is a sign, says **Andrew Huth**, of the shifting attitudes towards a composer once thought of as little more than a purveyor of nostalgic sentiment

The last time all of Rachmaninov's works for piano and orchestra were played at the Proms was 50 years ago. Back then audiences loved them, but critical attitudes were not so generous. In advanced musical circles a taste for Rachmaninov's music was barely respectable. The commonly held view of him during the last two decades of his life, and for many years afterwards, was of a magnificent pianist whose own music was sprawling, nostalgic and self-indulgent. People who distrusted the overt expression of emotion would feel embarrassed, even threatened, by it.

One reason why the picture has changed in the past half-century is simply that more of his music is played, and by leading musicians in fine performances. In the 1950s the only really familiar works were the Second and Third Piano Concertos, the *Paganini Rhapsody* and some of the solo piano music. Now that his orchestral works, his songs and choral music have become more familiar, Rachmaninov has been revealed as a deeper and more versatile figure, with a wider range of expression than he was credited with, and provoking more complex reactions in his listeners. The emotional nakedness has somehow become more acceptable, and so has the broad scale: it needs time to unfold and space to resonate in the mind.

Rachmaninov's style is recognisable in every bar he wrote. He wasn't the sort of composer who needed to push the boundaries of musical language: he accepted the late-Romantic style he inherited

> The commonly held view of Rachmaninov was of a magnificent pianist whose own music was sprawling, nostalgic and self-indulgent … The emotional nakedness of his music has now somehow become more acceptable.

and explored that territory again and again, treating similar ideas from different angles. Melody stands at the heart of his approach to composition, often with an improvisational quality that seems to reinvent itself bar after bar, as at the opening of the Second and Third Piano Concertos. Variations and reprises reveal new depths and new perspectives to ideas that at first seemed quite self-contained.

Many of Rachmaninov's melodic adventures begin with themes that recall the contours of folk music, the sound of bells so common in Russian music or the chants of the Orthodox Church. He remembered the singing of the St Petersburg church choirs as one of the most thrilling experiences of his childhood, and he later recreated that sense of excitement in one of the most remarkable choral works ever composed, his *All-Night Vigil* (1915), usually known as the *Vespers*. Written as the old Russia was descending into chaos, the *Vespers* is for many the quintessence of that rich, expressive choral sound unique to Russia.

For all its opulence, Rachmaninov's music often has a sense of fragility and loss. When he was still a child his improvident father lost the family money and estates. When he was 23 the First Symphony, in which he had invested so much care and passion, was given such an appalling performance that his confidence was shattered for years to come. In the first decade of the 20th century he regained a leading position among Russian composers with such

works as the Second and Third Piano Concertos, the Second Symphony, his choral symphony *The Bells* and the *Vespers*, but then came the 1917 Revolution. He lost everything when he left Russia to live in Western Europe and the USA.

The compositions from his years of reluctant exile develop and deepen the unchanging features of his style, but with a more acerbic harmonic sense and sharper melodic contours. This wasn't enough to satisfy Western listeners, who heard works like the *Paganini Rhapsody* and the *Symphonic Dances* as sad relics of a world that had disappeared for ever. Real Russian music, they felt, was being written by modernists like Stravinsky, Prokofiev and Shostakovich. In his own country, though, his music has almost always been valued for its expression of truths that don't depend on changing times and circumstances. It has now assumed even more importance as Russian culture is reforging links with a past and traditions that were so violently broken off in 1917. ●

Andrew Huth is a writer and translator working extensively in Russian, Eastern European and French music. He has produced subtitles for many Russian operas.

RACHMANINOV AT THE PROMS

24 July, Prom 10	Piano Concerto No. I
1 August, Prom 19	Symphonic Dances
4 August, Prom 24	Symphony No. 2; Prelude in C sharp minor, Op. 3 No. 2 (arr. Wood)
8 August, Prom 29	Rhapsody on a Theme of Paganini
11 August, Prom 34	Symphony No. 1
12 August, Prom 36	All-Night Vigil (Vespers)
23 August, Prom 49	Piano Concerto No. 4
30 August, Prom 59	Piano Concerto No. 3
31 August, Prom 60	Preludes – selection
6 September, Prom 69	Piano Concerto No. 2

RSC ROYAL SHAKESPEARE COMPANY

FROM 3 APRIL 2008

THE MERCHANT OF VENICE

THE TAMING OF THE SHREW

A MIDSUMMER NIGHT'S DREAM

HAMLET

LOVE'S LABOUR'S LOST

WILLIAM SHAKESPEARE

2008 STRATFORD-UPON-AVON SEASON

£5 TICKETS FOR 16-25 YEAR OLDS* *CONDITIONS APPLY

RSC TICKET HOTLINE 0844 800 1110

Photography from original production of *A Midsummer Night's Dream* by Stewart Hemley.

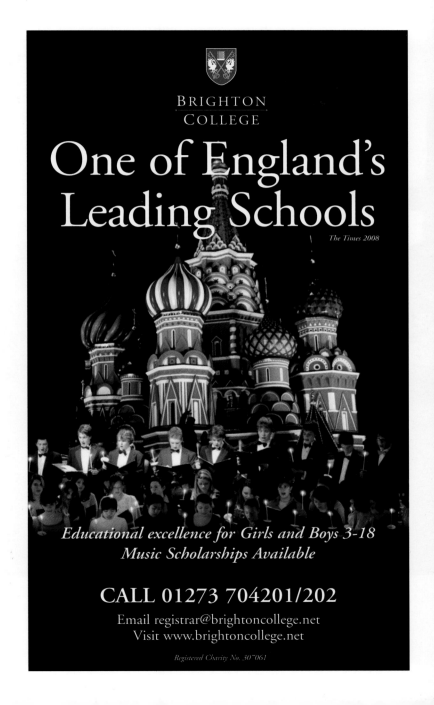

MODERNISM WITH SOUL

ELLIOTT CARTER (born 1908)

As the Proms marks the centenary of a latter-day American musical icon, **Arnold Whittall** reveals the human spirit beneath an uncompromising exterior

Elliott Carter was born in December 1908, just at the time when composers were beginning to explore those entirely new perspectives on tradition that marked music's advance into the bracing world of modernism. That same month saw the first performance, in Vienna, of Arnold Schoenberg's String Quartet No. 2, which had questioned the whole basis of melody and harmony as it had evolved over the centuries; and within a very few years, composers as different from Schoenberg as Stravinsky (*The Rite of Spring*) and Charles Ives (*Three Places in New England*) had shown that modernist initiatives could involve radically different styles and aesthetic approaches. This was a worldwide phenomenon, its impact felt in London and New York as well as in Paris and Vienna, and no composer has played a more fruitful and influential role in maintaining its values than Carter, with his commitment to music as a vehicle for imperishable, ever-aspiring human values.

In his early years, Carter was open-minded to a fault. But it took many years for him to find a personal voice within the welter of competing musical accents and dialects.

Schoenberg, Stravinsky and Ives all had significance for Carter: so did Debussy, among many others. But this year's Carter centenary would not be a cause for celebration had he not been able to pull free of his influences, while at the same time honouring those aspects of the great musical traditions which he admired so deeply. In his early years as a student and fledgling composer, Carter was open-minded to a fault. American-born, he was drawn to the iconoclasm of Ives, with whom he was personally acquainted; studying in Europe, he learnt much from the Stravinskyan enthusiasms of his teacher, Nadia Boulanger. But it took many years for him to find a personal voice within the welter of competing musical accents and dialects.

During the 1930s in America Carter began to carve out a career as a composer who, like Copland – another Boulanger pupil – held fast to certain long-standing conventions of harmony and form. His defining moment, setting him on the path he would follow consistently thereafter, did not come until after the Second World War. During 1950–51 he moved from New York City to the Sonora Desert near Tucson, Arizona, to work on his String Quartet No. 1. However, far from marking a decisive retreat from urban to pastoral, radical to conservative, this transformation reinforced the commitment to progressiveness that has sustained him ever since, in works ranging from the series of large-scale concertos to the concentrated miniatures of which *Caténaires* for solo piano is a recent example.

'Catenary' – the curve formed by a flexible cord, hanging freely between two points of support – is a design which Carter adopts to achieve coherence without relying on extensive use of literal repetition. But the coherence is expressive, not simply structural, and poetic ideas or visual images play a crucial role in helping to determine the character of his music – even when, as in the case of *A Symphony of Three Orchestras* (1976), they are not represented in the title. *Night Fantasies* (1980) for solo piano can be heard as an uninhibited depiction of how conflicting emotions and thoughts

alternately soothe and torment the wakeful would-be sleeper, the music's prodigal, spontaneous emotions and turbulent intensity carefully controlled but never awkwardly constrained.

Just as *Night Fantasies* saw a return to a genre – solo piano music – untouched by Carter since his Piano Sonata of almost 35 years earlier, so the Oboe Concerto (1987) rediscovered the formal principle he had most recently explored in the Piano Concerto more than 20 years before. Strong contrasts are no less vital here; but the prevailing mood is less anxious, more exuberant and, in the end, more serene than in *Night Fantasies*. Still more exuberant is the ten-minute *Soundings*, the miniature concerto for pianist/conductor which Carter wrote for Daniel Barenboim and the Chicago Symphony Orchestra in 2005, and in which some of the more exotic orchestral instruments – piccolos, contrabass clarinet and tuba – are also allowed to shine.

As all these works confirm, Carter's music is so memorable because, even when technically elaborate, it remains humane and deeply felt. Actively creating new works in his late nineties, one of the 20th century's most prolific – and enduring – masters has also helped lay the ground for distinctive musical developments in the decades to come. ●

Arnold Whittall has written extensively on 19th- and 20th-century music, in books ranging from *A Concise History of Romantic Music* to *Exploring Twentieth-Century Music* and *The Music of Britten and Tippett*. A former professor of King's College, London, he reviews regularly for *Gramophone* and *The Musical Times*.

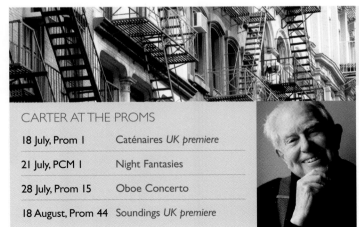

LEFT
Apartment blocks in New York City, where Carter was born

BELOW LEFT
Carter in 2005

CARTER AT THE PROMS

18 July, Prom 1	Caténaires UK premiere
21 July, PCM 1	Night Fantasies
28 July, Prom 15	Oboe Concerto
18 August, Prom 44	Soundings UK premiere

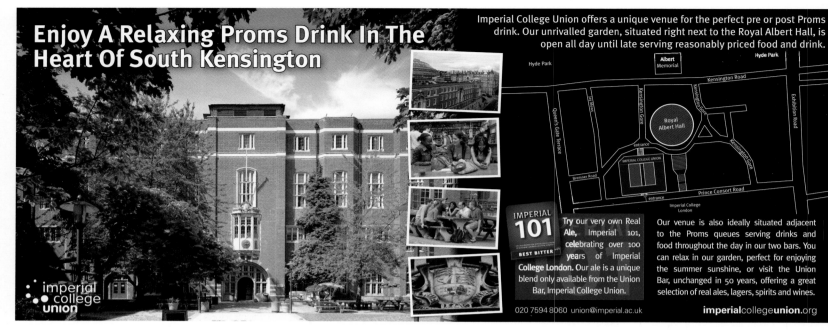

NEW MUSIC

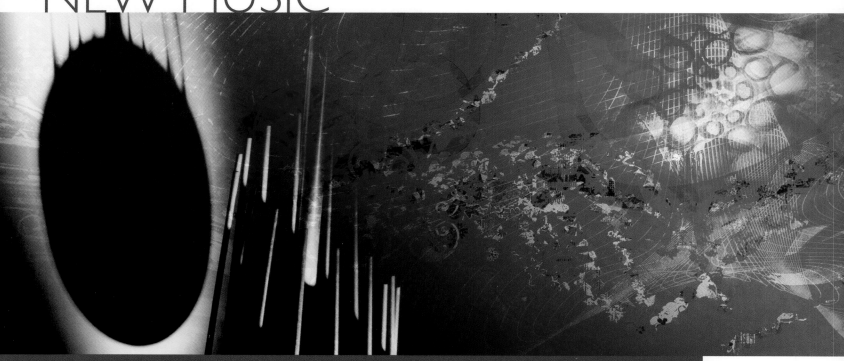

Since the days of Henry Wood, the Proms has been committed to new music, presenting the premieres of works by Schoenberg, Rimsky-Korsakov, Delius, Elgar, Bax and others. This year the Proms presents 11 BBC commissions and 9 UK premieres. **Ivan Hewett** introduces the season's range of new music – from Elliott Carter's fizzing First Night piano piece to Anna Meredith's Last Night nation-hopping – and reveals a rich range of inspiration, from the ill-fated *Columbia* space shuttle mission in 2003 to the limitless light of the sun

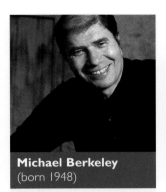

Michael Berkeley
(born 1948)

Slow Dawn
*world premiere
of new version*

The 'slow dawn' that lies behind this piece is not one but many spectacular dawns, seen by Michael Berkeley from the window of his Welsh country retreat. 'I love the way the light changes from total blackness to day, with many intermediate stages,' says Berkeley. But the piece's emotional gravity springs from the fact that it's also a memorial to the tragic, unexpected death of the son of a friend. And, beyond that, there's a connection to the opera Berkeley is now writing with novelist Ian McEwan. 'There's a "demonic" aria by a character expressing the idea that artistic creation has the scorching, dangerous power of the sun,' says Berkeley, 'and I think that feeling is in this piece too.'

PROM 33 Sunday 10 August

Elliott Carter
(born 1908)

Caténaires
UK premiere

In recent years Elliott Carter has seemed to be aiming at a new simplicity, particularly in the many works he's written for solo instruments. One might have expected Caténaires, written in 1998 for the pianist Pierre-Laurent Aimard, to reflect this trend. But Carter still has surprises up his sleeve. This is in fact an unabashedly virtuoso showpiece that hurtles along at top speed for its entire four-minute duration. The title refers to a 'catenary', which is the shape a cable makes when it hangs between two supports. Carter tells us that the work sprang out of an obsessive desire to make a piece out of a single running line, with no chords. The description sounds coolly abstract; the music is anything but.

PROM 1 Friday 18 July

Soundings
UK premiere

Elliott Carter is often thought of as unremittingly serious, but there's a rich vein of playfulness in his music. It's particularly evident in his contributions to the genre of the glittering American orchestral showpiece. This one was written in 2005 for Daniel Barenboim and the Chicago Symphony Orchestra. Carter's idea was to take 'soundings' of a myriad of different combinations of players 'and present them with good humour'. Many individual players have a chance to shine – including Barenboim himself, who was cast as both pianist and conductor. In the work's UK premiere at the Proms, the dual role is divided between conductor Ilan Volkov and pianist Nicolas Hodges, who will engage near the end in a teasing stop-start interplay.

PROM 44 Monday 18 August

Chen Yi
(born 1953)

Olympic Fire
*BBC commission:
world premiere*

Like many Chinese composers now in their fifties, Chen Yi was forced to give up her musical studies during the Chinese Cultural Revolution. But being forced into agricultural labour at least allowed her to discover the folk music of China's vast interior. It's a lesson she's not forgotten in her new life as an American citizen and professor at the University of Missouri-Kansas City. Her new piece celebrates the Olympic spirit, but it's not connected specifically to this year's games in Beijing. It looks forward to the London games in 2012 and, as she puts it, 'evokes the image of fire, not just as a physical power but as spiritual power. I also want to embody the idea of different cultures meeting and transforming.'

PROM 29 Friday 8 August

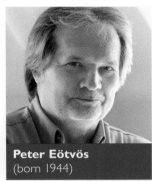

Peter Eötvös
(born 1944)

Seven
UK premiere

Hungarian composer Peter Eötvös has made a speciality of the concerto form: he's written five such pieces, including this one for violin. The title refers to the seven astronauts who perished in the Columbia space shuttle disaster of 2003. 'This is not a traditional concerto that sets up a contest or contrast between the soloist and the orchestra,' he says. 'It's a memorial piece, like Berg's Violin Concerto, and the orchestra's role is to create a sense of a vast space. It's as if the violin is travelling through this space as it sings.' The number seven is symbolised in many ways: there are 49 (ie 7x7) orchestral players, and six other violinists dotted around the auditorium, who act as satellites of the on-stage soloist.

PROM 55 Wednesday 27 August

MUSICIANS
BENEVOLENT FUND

listening to musicians – responding to their needs

For people in the music business there is always help at hand from the Musicians Benevolent Fund.

- Help with stress and health problems
- Help and advice with financial problems
- Help that's given in strict confidence
- Help given to outstanding young musicians

We operate throughout England, Scotland, Wales and the whole of Ireland.

If you or someone you know needs our help, please contact:

Musicians Benevolent Fund
16 Ogle Street
London
W1W 6JA

Tel: 020 7636 4481
Website: www.mbf.org.uk
Email: info@mbf.org.uk

Reg. Charity No. 228089

"A big thank you to all those who support our work so generously during the Proms season through the Promenaders' Musical Charities"

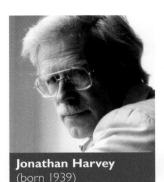

Jonathan Harvey
(born 1939)

Speakings
BBC co-commission with IRCAM and Radio France: UK premiere

Kenneth Hesketh
(born 1968)

Graven Image
BBC co-commission with Royal Liverpool Philharmonic Orchestra: world premiere

Anders Hillborg
(born 1954)

Clarinet Concerto
(Peacock Tales)
UK premiere

Simon Holt
(born 1958)

Troubled Light
BBC commission: world premiere

Magnus Lindberg
(born 1958)

Seht die Sonne
UK premiere

Harvey's new work for orchestra and live electronics is the final instalment of a trilogy written as Composer-in-Association of the BBC Scottish Symphony Orchestra. The Buddhist notions of purity in Body and Mind were the topics of the first two; now comes Speech. 'I've been fascinated by the connection between speech and music for years,' says Harvey. In this piece the orchestral sound is treated electronically, using powerful new speech-synthesis software. The spectacular result is the sound of instruments magically blended with vowels and consonants, as if the orchestra is learning to speak. 'But underlying the piece,' says the composer, 'is the ancient thought that there is a "pure speech", beyond language.'

Thoughts of mortality were in Hesketh's mind as he wrote this piece, prompted partly by the death of a friend's son – for whom this piece is a memorial. But it also reflects an abiding concern of Hesketh's, which is the mysterious borderline between the living and the mechanical. 'It's an uncanny aspect of the world, reflected in Romantic stories such as E. T. A. Hoffmann's *The Sandman*,' says Hesketh, 'and I wanted to capture that in this piece. It begins in a regular, mechanical way, like a series of clockwork escapements, then it becomes infected with irregularity. The end returns to regularity, but in a new way. It's an emotional journey, which came out much darker than I expected.'

Swedish composer Anders Hillborg found his voice when he abandoned purist modernism and embraced a happy eclecticism, in which the lyrical and the brutal, the hyperactive and the mysteriously still, live side by side. This piece begins with a long, ecstatically slow cantilena for the soloist, but soon becomes manically energetic. Hillborg was inspired to write this piece by the Swedish clarinettist Martin Fröst, who in this piece – and in this Proms performance – also draws upon his skills as a dancer and mime artist. But even on a purely musical level the clarinettist seems to be in a perpetual dance. 'I love the virtuosity of a great soloist like Martin,' says the composer. 'It gives us musical experiences that cannot be created in any other way.'

'Troubled light' was how Goethe described colour. Holt, too, is fascinated by colours, and how artists have used them. 'It's always an image that sets me going,' he says. 'I can't imagine writing a purely abstract orchestral piece.' There are five movements in *Troubled Light*, each prompted by a different colour. The title of the first, 'Fell of Dark', comes from Gerard Manley Hopkins; the second, 'Rudhira', is a 'two-minute flash of red'; 'Ellsworth' begins with a high-shimmering acid-yellow chord, inspired by an Ellsworth Kelly painting; then comes a moonstruck movement based on a line from Lorca; and finally 'Mehr Licht', which takes its title from Goethe's dying plea: 'More light'.

Finnish composer Magnus Lindberg used to be known as a composer of fiercely energetic orchestral 'soundscapes' that banished any sense of harmony or tonality. But recently a strain of luxuriant lyricism has emerged, and Lindberg now also makes references to familiar harmonies, though he's anxious to point out that 'the way of thinking is still atonal'. *Seht die Sonne* ('See the Sun') was written for Simon Rattle and the Berliner Philharmoniker, and was designed as a counterpart to Mahler's Ninth Symphony. 'The orchestral forces are identical to Mahler's – what a luxury that was!' he laughs. 'And my music begins with the same intervals. Later there's a reference to Schoenberg's *Gurrelieder*, where the soprano sings, "The sun shines." That gave me my title.'

PROM 45 Tuesday 19 August

PROM 19 Friday 1 August

PROM 37 Wednesday 13 August

PROM 11 Friday 25 July

PROM 59 Saturday 30 August

Malcolm Crowthers (Harvey); Mark McNulty (Hesketh); Betty Freeman/Lebrecht Music and Arts (Hillborg); Chris Christodoulou (Holt); Finnish Music Information Centre (Lindberg)

Stuart MacRae
(born 1976)

Gaudete
BBC commission:
world premiere

In an age when 'urban' styles of music are all the rage, Scottish composer Stuart MacRae's fascination with nature might seem somewhat old-fashioned. But there's no trace of nostalgia for a rural past in his uncompromisingly modernist vision. 'I am fascinated with mankind's relation to a nature that is completely indifferent to him,' he says. 'It can be nurturing and destructive and beautiful, all at once.' The focus of MacRae's new work is *Gaudete*, a collection of poems by Ted Hughes, a poet with a similar sense of nature's inscrutable otherness. 'I love the way Hughes gives us brilliant, sharp images of something unfathomable. I've chosen a group of poems from the collection's Epilogue that create a "life narrative" from birth to death.'

PROM 33 Sunday 10 August

Anna Meredith
(born 1978)

New work
BBC commission:
world premiere

The first commission for the Last Night of the Proms since 2003, Anna Meredith's new orchestral piece is, at the time of going to press, something of an unknown quantity. It may also incorporate other performers present at the Last Night, and there could be other musicians from further afield, beamed into the Hall from the Proms in the Park events taking place round the UK. If that's so, says Meredith, then all kinds of possibilities open up. There could be dialogues between orchestras hundreds of miles apart, perhaps even a rhythmic tossing back and forth of ideas, like a Medieval 'hocket'. But, however the details finally turn out, it's safe to say it will be brief, risky and exhilarating!

PROM 76 Saturday 13 September

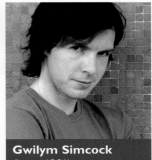

Gwilym Simcock
(born 1981)

Progressions
BBC commission:
world premiere

Britain is blessed with numerous young jazz piano talents but, by general consent, 27-year-old Gwilym Simcock is the brightest of them. He's the only jazz musician among the BBC New Generation Artists, and has been dubbed a 'creative genius' by no less than Chick Corea. His new work will be for his trio – which includes two other gifted musicians, drummer Martin France and bass player Phil Donkin – and the BBC Concert Orchestra. '*Progressions*,' explains Simcock 'is meant to bridge the gap between the traditional orchestral format and the contemporary improvisation of a piano trio.' The trick, he says, will be to combine classical discipline with jazz freedom. 'I want the listener to be unable to tell where the written-out part ends and the improvisation begins.'

PROM 31 Saturday 9 August

Steven Stucky
(born 1949)

Rhapsodies
BBC co-commission with
New York Philharmonic:
world premiere

Why *Rhapsodies*? 'Well, Lorin Maazel said to me, "Why don't you write something rhapsodic?",' says Steven Stucky with a laugh, aware that this might not seem the most carefully thought-out justification for a high-profile orchestral commission. But in fact Stucky gives the word 'rhapsody' a very particular twist. In this piece the word means not so much 'lyrically wayward' as 'maximally intense'. 'I want to create something that's at maximum heat for the whole of its length,' says Stucky. 'It's a continuously evolving single movement on the Sibelius model. It burns itself out in a series of waves, each starting out in one instrumental group and spreading out to the whole orchestra like a virus.'

PROM 57 Thursday 28 August

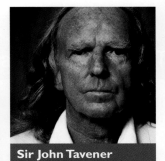

Sir John Tavener
(born 1944)

Cantus mysticus
UK premiere

John Tavener is well known for his long, slow, religiously inspired pieces, often based on Christian mystical writings. But lately his music has become more spiritually eclectic, mingling sources from several religious traditions. *Cantus mysticus* is an example of this trend. Scored for solo clarinet, soprano and string orchestra, it's short by Tavener's standards, being only seven minutes long. But there's time to hear lines from Goethe, Dante and from Buddhist scriptures, linked by the idea of the creative Feminine element in the Divine. The music rises in pitch and intensity, with echoes of birdsong in the dialogue between voice and clarinet. At the climax the clarinet bursts into a wild jazz improvisation, representing the principle of *lîla* (divine play).

PROM 56 Wednesday 27 August

The Sage Gateshead is an international home for music and musical discover

The Sage Gateshead occupies one of the most dramatic urban sites in Europe, on the River Tyne. It houses performance spaces of acoustic excellence with state-of-the art facilities, quality catering, licensed bars and excellent road, rail and air links.

"With its breathtaking Foster architecture, revolutionary intermingling of educational, community and professional music-making, and passionate support from Gateshead Council, The Sage Gateshead has quickly become the most exciting music venue in Britain – and Northern Sinfonia has raised its game to match its new home." The Times

For further details contact The Sage Gateshead's Performance Programme Co-ordinator on +44 (0) 191 443 4666 or e-mail HallBookings@thesagegateshead.org

Hall One

Hall Two

Northern Sinfonia
50th Anniversary Season
Music Director, Thomas Zehetmair

Northern Sinfonia, orchestra of The Sage Gateshead

The Sage Gateshead's 2008/09 Classical Subscription Series incorporates Northern Sinfonia's 50th Anniversary Season. Subscription packages offering substantial savings and other benefits go on sale in May; tickets for individual concerts in the series go on sale in June. Call 0191 443 4661 or visit www.thesagegateshead.org for a brochure.

To discuss booking Northern Sinfonia contact Simon Clugston, Performance Programme Director on +44 (0) 191 443 4666 or e-mail simon.clugston@thesagegateshead.org

Gateshead Council
www.gateshead.gov.uk

ARTS COUNCIL ENGLAND

Photography: Alex Telfer, Richard Bryant

Mark-Anthony Turnage
(born 1960)

Chicago Remains
UK premiere

The Torino Scale
UK premiere

Huw Watkins
(born 1976)

Sad Steps
BBC commission:
world premiere

Jason Yarde
(born 1970)

Rhythm and Other
Fascinations
BBC commission:
world premiere

Hanya Chlala/ArenaPal (Turnage); Hanya Chlala (Watkins); BBC (Yarde)

British composer Mark-Anthony Turnage, now in his late forties, has often been inspired by American themes and American music, particularly jazz. This piece, which was premiered last October by the Chicago Symphony Orchestra and Bernard Haitink, is inspired by the city of Chicago, though Turnage disclaims any influence from the jazz and blues of that city. 'It was the architecture that really struck me,' he says. 'It's such an amazingly beautiful city.' The majesty of the cityscape has left its mark on the music's quietly massive sound-world. Chicago poet Carl Sandburg, who famously described the meat-loving city as 'Hog Butcher for the World' and 'City of the Big Shoulders', also helped Turnage to focus the character of this broad, slow, lyrical piece.

The Torino Scale has nothing to do with Italian music – it's a measure of the hazard posed to our planet by 'near-Earth' objects such as asteroids. Mark-Anthony Turnage first became involved with these mysterious objects when he was asked to contribute a new movement to Simon Rattle's recording of Holst's *The Planets*. Composing *Ceres*, named after the largest of the asteroids, sparked off a fascination for what Turnage calls 'the doomsday aspect of asteroids, which could destroy Earth one day'. Since then he's written *Juno*, and now *The Torino Scale*, both premiered by the Bamberg Symphony Orchestra and Jonathan Nott. The material takes its cue from the musical connotations of the title, and Turnage describes the piece as 'only little, but a bit wild'.

Welsh composer Huw Watkins is only in his thirties, but already he's amassed an astonishingly large catalogue of works – many of them involving himself as a pianist. This septet is written for the Aronowitz Ensemble, a group the composer has known for years. 'I always like to write for players I know,' says Watkins. 'The title is a phrase from a poem in Philip Larkin's *The Whitsun Weddings*. The piece is for an unusual ensemble of six strings and piano, and thus far it's emerging as a *concertante* piece, with the piano set against the strings, rather than woven in with them. The title reflects the rather sombre mood of the work, which I think will be a sequence of sad, but dance-like, pieces.'

Jason Yarde is best known as the brilliant alto sax player and composer who led the ground-breaking Jazz Warriors band. But he's no stranger to the orchestral world. Along with Charles Hazlewood, the BBC Concert Orchestra and the producer DaVinChe he created the ground-breaking 'Urban Classics' project, which married orchestral sound, jazz idioms and the specifically British urban music known as 'grime'. His new work, he says, will grow out of that experience, but with a new element added to the mix: 'I love the way Gershwin spans the pop and orchestral worlds, and I really wanted to create something that would pay homage to that.'

PROM 71 Monday 8 September

PROM 13 Sunday 27 July

PCM 8 Monday 8 September

PROM 31 Saturday 9 August

Further premieres

Arnold Bax (1883–1953)
In memoriam Patrick Pearse
First public performance
PROM 10 Thursday 24 July

Karlheinz Stockhausen
(1928–2007)

Klang, 5th hour – Harmonien
for solo trumpet
BBC commission: world premiere

Klang, 13th hour – Cosmic
Pulses
UK premiere
PROM 20 Saturday 2 August

New arrangements

Chris Hazell (born 1948)
Folk-song medley
BBC commission: world premiere
PROM 76 Saturday 13 September

Kathryn Tickell (born 1967)
New arrangement
BBC commission: world premiere
PROM 4 Sunday 20 July

Jason Yarde (born 1970)
Gershwin Porgy and Bess –
'My man's gone now'
BBC commission: world premiere
PROM 31 Saturday 9 August

Orchestrations of Schubert
songs, by:

Detlev Glanert (born 1960)
Colin Matthews (born 1946)
David Matthews (born 1943)
Manfred Trojahn (born 1949)
BBC commissions:
world premieres
PROM 48 Friday 22 August

BBC Philharmonic

Painting by Gwyn

"*Gianandrea Noseda obtains superlative orchestral playing which is captured by the excellent recording (Mahler 10 - Chandos) and the symphony's hypnotic power is projected with the surest of touches. The scherzos are especially characterised and the interpretation of the devastating finale is - well, devastating.*"
Michael Kennedy, The Sunday Telegraph, February 08

Widely recognised as one of Britain's finest orchestras, the BBC Philharmonic is based in Manchester where it performs regularly at the magnificent Bridgewater Hall. It also records programmes and concerts for Radio 3, has an exclusive recording contract with Chandos Records and an extensive outreach and community programme.

Gianandrea Noseda	Chief Conductor
Vassily Sinaisky	Chief Guest Conductor
James MacMillan	Composer/Conductor
Sir Edward Downes	Conductor Emeritus
Yan Pascal Tortelier	Conductor Laureate
Yuri Torchinsky	Leader

BBC Philharmonic
t. 0161 244 4001
e. philharmonic@bbc.co.uk
w. bbc.co.uk/philharmonic

BBC RADIO 3
90 – 93FM

Supported by
Salford City Council

"A world class music festival" BBC Music Magazine

PRAGUE

www.praguewinter.com

THE 2009 PRAGUE WINTER FESTIVAL

For five days in January at the beginning of every year the capital of the Czech Republic comes alive with the Prague Winter Festival. Celebrating its 37th year in 2009, the festival continues to go from strength to strength. At night, there is the chance to enjoy performances of classical music, opera and ballet in some of Europe's most beautifully ornate venues; whilst by day, you can enjoy performances by the world famous Bambini di Praga, Black Light Theatre, plus there are a number of day tours to choose from visiting places such as Bertramka, Karlstejn Castle or Vysoka, the charming village which was the inspiration for Dvořák's Rusalka.

Packages include

- Return flights to Prague
- 3, 4 or 5 nights in a 4* or 5* hotel with buffet breakfast
- Opening ceremony
- Choice of 3 evening performances (E)
- Choice of 2 daytime options (D)
- Closing ceremony
- Festival welcome pack on arrival
- Comprehensive festival guide

2009 PROGRAMME
*Pre-bookable optional extras

Friday 02 January	20:00	Don Giovanni (by Mozart) in Estates Theatre (E)
	20:00	Swan Lake (ballet by Tchaikovsky) in Prague State Opera (E)
	20:00	5-course dinner with music in the Mlynec Michelin starred restaurant (E)
Saturday 03 January	11.30	Festival Opening Ceremony
	14:00	City Tour (Option 1: Walking Tour or Option 2: Coach Tour) (D)
	15:00	Black Light Theatre (D)
	20:00	La Bohème (G.Puccini) in the State Opera (E)
	20:00	The Nutcracker (ballet by Tchaikovsky) in National Theatre (E)
Sunday 04 January	09:00	Half-day tour to Kutna Hora*
	12:00	Villa Bertramka*
	15:00	Hradistan Dulcimer Band (D)
	20:00	The Flying Dutchman (Wagner) with buffet after performance in the Prague State Opera (E)
Monday 05 January	09:00	Day Tour to Vysoka and Dvořák's House (D)
	15:00	Bambini di Praga (D)
	19:30	Czech Philharmonic Orchestra, Dvořák Hall, Rudolfinum (E)
	19:00	5-course dinner with music in the Mlynec Michelin starred restaurant (E)
	21:45	Festival Closing Ceremony
Tuesday 06 January	09:00	Half day tour to Karlstejn Castle & Nizbor*
	19:00	Turnadot (G.Puccini) in the Prague State Opera (E)
	20:00	5-course dinner with music in the Mlynec Michelin starred restaurant (E)

ifb

PRICES

Twin/Double pps	4*	5*	Single pp	4*	5*
3 nights from	£395	£458	3 nights from	£468	£550
4 nights from	£423	£501	4 nights from	£520	£624
5 nights from	£451	£544	5 nights from	£572	£698

tax & insurance not included

ATOL 3198

ABTA V2452

Reservations & Enquiries
CALL 0870 247 1204

THE PROMMING EXPERIENCE

As he enters his third decade of Promming (he started young!), **Nick Breckenfield** explains the ins and outs of standing up for music, and offers a view from the Arena

Despite the impression you might glean from the television coverage of the Last Night, those of us who crowd the Royal Albert Hall's Arena and Gallery each summer at the Proms don't dress up every night and wave balloons. For the 70-plus concerts before the Last Night, we're just ordinary folk with a passion for music.

Prommers come from all walks of life – name a profession and there's likely to be a Prommer from it – and while that alone might not distinguish us from other classical music audiences, it's the unique sense of informality that enables us to mix more freely and creates a sense of community. Being on your feet somehow also makes you hear differently: you're transformed from being a passive listener to an active one, with every sinew responding to the sheer physical sound of what could be more than 100 musicians playing right in front of you.

As a Prommer, you can get into any concert – even the Last Night – for only £5.00. There's also the satisfaction of knowing that Promming – or 'Promenading' (early Proms audiences were able to stroll around during the concerts) – is, after all, what gave this great festival its name.

Arena or Gallery?

The main choice a new Prommer has to make is where to stand. There are two Promming areas – the Arena (the large space in the centre of the auditorium) or the Gallery (directly in front of the stage), with its bird's-eye view of proceedings. Down in the Arena you are a little more on show (could the Prommers here be just a touch more extrovert?), but when the performance starts, everyone's concentration is on the music. Without a doubt, this is where you can get closest to the performers, many of whom have complimented the attentiveness of the Arena crowd.

The Gallery experience is not only spectacularly atmospheric, with the brightly lit performers on stage seeming like a distant galaxy emitting heavenly music, but it is even more relaxed, with some Prommers spreading out, reading a book or newspaper, and disappearing into their own, beautifully accompanied dream-world. Former Proms director Nicholas Kenyon jestingly suggested to the *New York Times* last year that 'the Gallery is a law unto itself. We hear strange stories about what goes on. We even believe that babies have been born up there or, if not born, at least conceived.'

The 'party' line

Part of the fun of Promming is the genuine camaraderie, which undoubtedly starts before the concert, in the queue. All Promming tickets (unless you have a Season Ticket or a Weekend Promming Pass, see pages 57 & 136) are sold only on the day of the concert, from up to an hour before the start-time. While the two so-called 'Day' queues for tickets (one queue each for Arena and Gallery Prommers, at Doors 11 and 10 respectively) spill out to the west, the season-ticket holders (Door 1 for Arena, Door 2 for Gallery) queue to the east. Even for very popular concerts, it's unlikely you'll be turned away, but the earlier you arrive, the better your chance of gaining a coveted position near the front of your chosen Promming area.

As befits a nation renowned for queuing, there is a raffle-ticket numbering system run by the Hall's stewards if you want to return to your place in the queue after attending a Proms Plus pre-concert event (see pages 70–72 & 91–127); the system also operates on days when there is more than one concert. If you just need to nip off to the loo, neighbours in the queue are usually happy to let you back in.

Take your place

Once you've paid, you either descend into the Arena or climb up to the Gallery (which is also wheelchair accessible). You can, of course, take your place anywhere, providing no-one has taken that space before you. Mostly, people fill up from the front.

All you have to do now is enjoy the music. The Proms are renowned both for their quality and variety, and you can be sure that you'll be hearing thoroughly prepared performances. I'd always recommend buying a printed programme, as they flesh out the context to the pieces and make the listening even more enjoyable.

Dress and comfort

Though some choose to don best bib and tucker for the Last Night, in case they're picked up by the TV cameras, the Proms has no dress code. Wear what's comfortable, and remember that on a busy night it can get pretty warm in the Arena. A bottle of water is handy, too, either for when it gets too warm, or if you feel a throat tickle coming on. ▶

ABOVE
Standing up for music: Prommers at the Last Night, watched by listeners in the Stalls seating area

BELOW
The central attraction: Arena Prommers soaking up the atmosphere

Chris Christodoulou (all photos)

POINTS FOR PROMMERS

- The most popular concerts will attract the biggest crowds, so queue early for these – especially if you want to be near the front of the Arena (not necessarily the best place acoustically)

- If you're happy to stand further back in the Arena, you can usually get away with turning up half an hour before the start-time

- In general, there's more space to spread out in the Gallery than in the Arena

- On hot days it may be useful to bring a bottle of water

- Make the most of queuing – bring a book, a game or a picnic – or make friends with your neighbours

- If you're not sure where to queue – ask a steward (easily identified by their red coats)

"They stamp their feet in time to the hornpipe – that is until I whip up the orchestra in a fierce *accelerando* which leaves behind all those whose stamping technique is not of the very first quality. I like to win by two bars, if possible; but sometimes have to be content with a bar-and-a-half."

Sir Henry Wood on his annual race with the Promenaders in his *Fantasia on British Sea-Songs*, a Last Night staple

Next steps

If you get the Promming bug, then you might in future consider a Whole or Half-Season Ticket, which (if you go to all the concerts) can bring the price down to less than £2.25 a pop – one of the best bargains in classical music. But there are also Weekend Promming Passes, which give you access (via the Season Ticket-holder queues, no less!) to Friday-to-Sunday concerts, if any weekends particularly catch your eye (see page 136).

Whole Season Tickets automatically include entry to the Last Night, and Half-Season Ticket-holders have access to a special allocation of Last Night Promming tickets (see page 137).

Traditions and rituals

It's no surprise that certain Promenaders' traditions have built up over the 113-year-history of the Proms. Some of them poke fun at 'normal' concert-going etiquette. When, for instance, the piano lid is raised by the stagehands prior to a concerto performance, the Arena Prommers shout, 'Heave', and the Gallery answers, 'Ho'. Then, when the orchestra's leader steps up to the keyboard to sound an 'A', for the orchestra to tune to, mock applause bursts forth in praise of this brief performance. Less mischievously, in recent years, foreign orchestras have been greeted with a welcome in their own language. These little routines are all part of the fun and you don't have to join in – but the Proms certainly wouldn't be the same without them.

The Prommers' keen sense of loyalty to the festival is reflected in the daily charity collection that has become a feature, with front-row Prommers collecting for music-related charities. Last year over £67,000 was raised – averaging over £1,000 for each day of the Proms season. And touchingly, during every Last Night concert, when it comes to laying a wreath around the bronze bust of Sir Henry Wood (founder-conductor of the Proms), the duty falls to a pair of representatives drawn from the Prommers – another symbol of how those thronged in the Arena and Gallery are central to the Proms experience. ●

Nick Breckenfield is Classical Music and Opera Editor for www.whatsonwhen.com. He writes programme notes for the International Piano Series at the Southbank Centre and for the Hong Kong Sinfonietta, among others.

Chris Christodoulou

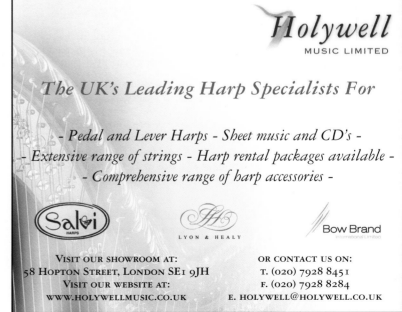

Promming at a glance

What is Promming?

The popular tradition of Promming is central to the unique and informal atmosphere of the BBC Proms at the Royal Albert Hall.

Up to 1,400 standing places are available at each Proms concert. The traditionally low prices allow you to enjoy world-class concerts for just £5.00 each (or even less with a Season Ticket or Weekend Promming Pass). There are two standing areas: the Arena, located directly in front of the stage, and the Gallery, running round the top of the Hall. All spaces are unreserved.

Day Prommers

Over 500 Arena and Gallery tickets (priced £5.00) go on sale 30 minutes before doors open (one hour before on days when there are Proms Plus pre-concert events to allow Prommers to attend these events). These tickets cannot be booked in advance, so even if all seats have been sold, you always have a good chance of getting in (though early queuing is advisable for the more popular concerts). You must buy your ticket in person, and must pay by cash.

Wheelchair-users who wish to Prom (Gallery only) should queue in the same way but will be redirected to Door 8 once their ticket is purchased. (For further information for disabled concert-goers, see page 135.)

Day tickets are available (for cash only) at Door 11 (Arena) and Door 10 (Gallery), not at the Box Office. If you are in doubt about where to go, Royal Albert Hall stewards will point you in the right direction.

Prommers' Season Tickets

Frequent Prommers can save money by purchasing Arena or Gallery Season Tickets covering either the whole Proms season (including the Last Night) or only the first or second half (*ie* Proms 1–39 or Proms 40–75, excluding the Last Night).

Season Ticket-holders benefit from:

- guaranteed entrance (until 10 minutes before each concert)
- great savings – prices can work out at less than £2.25 per concert
- guaranteed entrance to the Last Night for Whole Season Ticket-holders and special access to a reserved allocation of Last Night tickets for Half-Season Ticket-holders (see page 137).

Please note that Season Ticket-holders arriving at the Hall less than 10 minutes before a concert are not guaranteed entry and may be asked, in certain circumstances, to join the day queue.

Please note that Season Tickets are non-transferable; two passport-sized photographs must be provided before tickets can be issued. Season Tickets are not valid for concerts at Cadogan Hall.

For further details and prices of Season Tickets, see page 139. You can also buy Weekend Promming Passes – see page 136 for details.

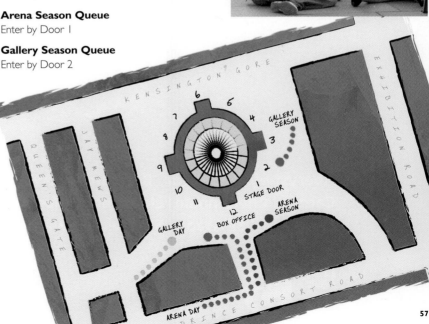

Where to Queue

- **Arena Day Queue**
  Enter by Door 11
- **Gallery Day Queue**
  Enter by Door 10
- **Arena Season Queue**
  Enter by Door 1
- **Gallery Season Queue**
  Enter by Door 2

Chris Christodoulou

BBC National Orchestra of Wales

Cerddorfa Genedlaethol Gymreig y BBC

2008 - 2009 Concert Season

"..the Welsh orchestra, conducted by Thierry Fischer, was outstanding from the downbeat." **Washington Post**

"the second-half performance ...for want of better words, simply blew me away." **Western Mail**

Aberystwyth | **Bangor** | **Bradford-on-Avon** | **Brecon** **Cardiff** | **Cheltenham** | **Llandudno** | **Monmouth** **Newtown** | **St Asaph** | **St Davids** | **Swansea** | **Wrexham**

Call FREE for details of all our 2008/09 concerts BBC National Orchestra of Wales Audience Line:

0800 052 1812

bbc.co.uk/now

BBC RADIO 3

90 – 93FM

BBC Cymru Wales

GLYNDEBOURNE
ON TOUR 2008

G Bizet
CARMEN
A revival of David McVicar's 2002 Festival production

W A Mozart
THE MAGIC FLUTE
A revival of Adrian Noble's 2004 Festival production

E Humperdinck
HÄNSEL UND GRETEL
A new production from the 2008 Festival
directed by Laurent Pelly

GLYNDEBOURNE ON TOUR 2008

GLYNDEBOURNE	14 October – 1 November
WOKING	4 – 8 November
STOKE-ON-TRENT	11 – 15 November
MILTON KEYNES	18 – 22 November
NORWICH	25 – 29 November
PLYMOUTH	2 – 6 December

To join our FREE tour mailing list and receive full
details of the 2008 Tour, please call 01273 815000
or email info@glyndebourne.com
or write to: GOT Mailing List, Glyndebourne,
Lewes, East Sussex, BN8 5UU

www.glyndebourne.com

GLYNDEBOURNE ON TOUR...
A YOUTHFUL & VIBRANT JOURNEY
SUNDAY INDEPENDENT

ALL TOGETHER NOW ...

From folk dancing to family orchestras, from family-friendly Music Intro events to opportunities for young composers, this year's Proms Learning projects are designed to get even more people involved in the experience of live music-making. **Harriet Smith** is your guide through the rich offerings

Perhaps the biggest challenge facing the Proms Learning team this year was how to top last year's bonanza – in particular the resounding success of Brass Day, which explored the glories of all things brass, from the ancient nine-foot-long Uzbek *karnay* (trumpet) to the finest exponents of our own great brass-band tradition, not forgetting the many young players experiencing the thrill of ensemble playing for the first time.

The solution? In a departure from the highly successful recent day-long celebrations devoted to individual instruments or instrumental families – the violin, the voice and brass – this year's focus will be on the broader theme of folk music, which reflects the Proms' anniversary celebration of Vaughan Williams, himself an avid collector of folk songs. If the idea of folk music in this country once conjured up clichéd images of men in funny hats, today it's a tradition gaining ground among people of all ages.

Folk Day

The aim of the Proms Folk Day (Sunday 20 July) is to involve as many different aspects of the folk world as can be squeezed into a single day – including playing, singing, dancing and composing. Geographically, the emphasis will be on the British Isles, with ebullient group Muzsikás from Hungary adding an Eastern European tang. Young players from Folkestra, the folk music organisation based at The Sage in Gateshead, will lead the British contingent.

Whether you've already got the folk bug or you want to explore a whole new area of music, the two main concerts of this year's Folk Day will offer the perfect showcase of some of the finest musicians around. As with last year's Brass Day, there'll also be opportunities to get involved. The morning will focus on large-scale group events open to all, including a workshop with the Proms Folk Family Chorus, in which you can join up to 400 fellow singers to learn new folk-song arrangements. Or, if you have an instrument you want to bring along, you can join the Proms Folk Family Orchestra (see box below right).

If you'd rather spectate than participate, in the afternoon the lawns surrounding the bandstand in Kensington Gardens will thrill to the sound of story-telling, small folk ensembles and even maypole dancing, in the Proms' very own mini folk festival – Proms Folk in the Park. Those who've taken part in the morning workshop will also get to demonstrate the fruits of their labours, presenting Folk Day to the wider world in rousing style.

There will also be two concerts – starting at 3.30pm and 7.30pm – in the Hall itself (see Listings, page 93). In the afternoon, young musicians get to work alongside professional players in another very successful Proms Learning venture, Side by Side. The London Sinfonietta, plus young players, will be joined by Muzsikás and Folkestra, and the concert will end in a grand finale, bringing all of the performers together. The evening concert brings a folk gig centred around singer/concertina player Bella Hardy, guitarist/singer Martin Simpson and the group Bellowhead. As if that were not enough, the night will be rounded off with the Proms' first ever ceilidh, so be sure to bring along your dancing shoes! ▶

ABOVE & BELOW
A festival spirit and quiet captivation at family events during last year's Proms

---

Fancy being part of Folk Day on Sunday 20 July?

Proms Folk Family Chorus and Orchestra
10am–12noon

If you love singing and you'd enjoy learning some new folk songs, sign up for the Proms Folk Family Chorus. Or the Proms Folk Family Orchestra might be more your kind of thing. Both these events take place from 10am to 12noon in South Kensington, and will be showcased at Proms Folk in the Park.

For information about taking part in either of these events, please visit bbc.co.uk/proms, email promslearning@bbc.co.uk or call 020 7765 2679

Proms Folk in the Park
12noon–3pm, Kensington Gardens

A free Proms mini folk festival in the park. Bring your family and a picnic, and enjoy a variety of folk performances and activities before the afternoon's free concert.

For more information, visit bbc.co.uk/proms

Proms Folk Day: FREE concert
3.30pm–c6.00pm, Royal Albert Hall

Prom 4 is a free event. Tickets will be available from the Royal Albert Hall Box Office (in person, online at bbc.co.uk/proms or by phone – 0845 401 5040*) from **Monday 30 June**. *Calls from a BT landline are charged at local rate. Charges from mobiles or other networks may be higher.*

"The first thing my son Jake did when he got home from Brass Day was to get out his trumpet to practise, so if the aim of Brass Massive was to inspire young players, then it was a great success. Please do it again!"

Steve Dix Proms Brass Day 2007

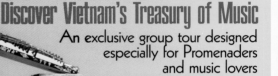

"It was inspiring, uplifting and wonderful food for the soul. Thank you, thank you, thank you."

Rachelle Howard Out+About 2007

Out+About

It's remarkable how rapidly a bright idea can take hold and spread. Out+About is one of those concepts that has expanded beyond recognition. The premise is simple: just think of Mohammed and the mountain. Rather than trying to lure people into the Royal Albert Hall (there's plenty of that already at the Proms), the musicians of the BBC Symphony Orchestra will take to the streets and provide instant tasters of classical music, everywhere from shopping centres to railway concourses. After last year's events at the Brighton Dome, this year the focus is firmly back on London, and on Thursday 26 June chamber groups from brass ensembles to string quartets will be found performing for free around London in some very unexpected locations. To find out more visit bbc.co.uk/proms.

Music Intro

Another idea that has caught the imagination of Proms audiences is Music Intro. This year seven Proms concerts have been selected for the Music Intro treatment – which offers a specially devised pre-concert introduction to families, giving them the opportunity to have a sneak preview of the works themselves, meet the players and hear the stories behind the music. These family-friendly musical appetisers continue to be a central feature of the Proms Learning events, so whether you want to know more about the music of Czech composers Smetana and Dvořák (7 August), the jazz-inflected works of Bernstein, Gershwin and Stravinsky (9 August) or the symphonic worlds of Brahms and Shostakovich (3 September), there'll be something to tickle your musical tastebuds in a relaxed yet informative way (see 'Dates for your Diary' box, page 67).

Music Intro now joins the greatly extended range of other free pre-Prom events under the umbrella title of Proms Plus, all under one roof at the Royal College of Music's Britten Theatre (see page 70–72). For other family-friendly events, see 'Dates for your Diary' box, page 67). ▶

ABOVE
Another string to her bow: a young player at one of last year's Proms Family Orchestra workshops

BELOW
How did they do *that*? The audience of tomorrow at last year's Out+About concert in Brighton

"What a fantastic event. A huge thank you for giving so many people in Brighton such a wonderful musical opportunity. Everyone just loved being involved. The children and staff here have been talking about nothing else all day!"

Downs Junior School, Brighton Out+About 2007

Chris Christodoulou (above right and bottom)

Lowell Libson Ltd

British paintings watercolours & drawings
17th to 20th century

3 Clifford Street · London W1S 2LF
Telephone: + 44 (0)20 7734 8686
Email: pictures@lowell-libson.com
Fax: +44 (0)20 7734 9997
www.lowell-libson.com

George Romney *Titania's Attendants* · painted *c.*1792 · oil on canvas · 47 × 59 in.

Inspire – a feast for young composers

BBC Proms Inspire – the scheme for young composers – continues to go from strength to strength. If ever anything were designed to banish the idea of the composer working in an ivory tower, cut off from reality, this is it. Inspire is all about creation and collaboration. At its centre is the BBC Proms Inspire Young Composers' Competition, which is followed by workshops where winning composers get to hear their music brought to life, and to discuss it with their fellow composers and with the players themselves. Last year's competition offered the five winners a professional commission for a chamber work. Each of them was given a slightly different brief, and an unorthodox instrumental line-up to tackle. Earlier this year the five composers came together to hear their finished pieces recorded by professional BBC musicians. The pieces will be performed again (complete with a broadcast on BBC Radio 3) in a special Proms Plus event on Saturday 26 July. And at the Inspire Day on Wednesday 6 August, you can hear the pieces by 2008's five winners, before they get on with writing their own new commissions for next year.

So if you're a keen composer, aged between 12 and 18, you have until Friday 23 May to get your entry in for next year's Inspire Young Composers' Competition – and the chance to take your composing to the next level (see box below). ▶

"The improvisation sessions were great and have opened my mind to a different way of composing and making music."

Inspire Day 2007

INTO THE GROOVE:
A session at a week-long summer academy last year in preparation for a Proms performance

INSPIRE

Do you know someone who should be entering the BBC Proms Inspire Young Composers' Competition, for 12- to 18-year-olds?

The deadline for entries is Friday 23 May 2008.

The 2008 Inspire Day, including the Young Composers' Concert at the Britten Theatre, Royal College of Music, will be held on Wednesday 6 August.

For more details, visit bbc.co.uk/proms, email promslearning@bbc.co.uk or call 020 7765 2679

Proms Family Orchestra

On the surface the idea of seasoned professionals getting together with amateur family performers might seem a recipe for disaster. But the Proms Family Orchestra has already proved this is anything but the case. It first came into being in 2006, when five people turned up at a primary school in Reading for the first rehearsal. More recent Proms Family Orchestras have become bigger than your average symphony orchestra, featuring a wide range of music, and an even wider range of ages. The idea is to give family members – whether mums, dads, brothers, sisters, aunts, uncles or grandparents – the chance to play music together. Everyone is welcome, from keen amateurs to those who've never played in an orchestra before. This year the composer Errollyn Wallen, fittingly described in *The Observer* as a 'renaissance woman of contemporary British music', will be writing a new work that is sufficiently flexible in its scoring to be effective, whatever forces come together in each incarnation of the family orchestra (see box right). Every performance will be a unique event, and it's that spirit of music being a living, breathing entity that lies at the heart of the Proms. ●

Following periods as Editor of *BBC Music Magazine* and *International Record Review*, Harriet Smith combines her passions for music and gardening as a freelance journalist, editor and broadcaster.

"It was the first time my son had played with more than one other person and he was over the moon. The first question he asked on the way out was 'Can we do that again?' Many thanks to the 'real' musicians, who were great, both with the kids and the adults."

Tina Eager
Proms Family Orchestra 2007

DATES FOR YOUR DIARY

Music Intro
Britten Theatre, Royal College of Music

7 August, Prom 28	5.45pm–6.30pm
9 August, Prom 31	5.15pm–6.00pm
23 August, Prom 49	4.45pm–5.30pm
27 August, Prom 55	5.15pm–6.00pm
31 August, Prom 60	2.15pm–3.00pm
1 September, Prom 62	5.15pm–6.00pm
3 September, Prom 65	5.30pm–6.30pm

Free to ticket-holders for the evening concert

Proms Family Orchestra
Britten Theatre, Royal College of Music (except * Royal Albert Hall)

20 July	10.00am–12.00noon
27 July	2.00pm–4.00pm
9 August	2.00pm–4.00pm
25 August	11.30am–1.30pm & *2.30pm–4.30pm
30 August	2.00pm–4.00pm

Free. *To book places please visit bbc.co.uk/proms, email promslearning@bbc.co.uk or call 020 7765 2679*

Look out, too, for other family-friendly Proms and events: Doctor Who Prom (27 July), Lang Lang (31 August) and Literary Festival events on 20 July and 12 August. See Listings (pages 92–127) for details.

Simon Jay Price

BBC Concert ORCHESTRA

The heart of great music

Be the first to hear about our events and broadcasts

Join the BBC Concert Orchestra free mailing list.
Email, text or call us with your contact details:

Email **concert.orch@bbc.co.uk**
Text **BBC CO to 83111**
Call **020 8752 4676**

bbc.co.uk/concertorchestra

WIGMORE HALL

WIGMORE SERIES
20082009

SEPTEMBER 08 – JULY 09

Including concerts by ...
Radu Lupu | **Steven Isserlis** | Thomas Adès | **Emerson String Quartet**
Paul Lewis | **Mitsuko Uchida** | Ysaÿe Quartet | **Jerusalem Quartet**
Florestan Trio | **Midori** | Truls Mørk | **Till Fellner** | Joshua Bell | **Kate Royal**
Joyce DiDonato | **András Schiff** | Steven Osborne | **Alice Coote**
Belcea Quartet | **Andreas Scholl** | Christoph Eschenbach | **Thomas Quasthoff**
Julia Fischer | **Academy of Ancient Music** | Gabrieli Consort & Players
Les Talens Lyriques | Colin Currie | **Richard Goode** | The King's Consort
... and many more of the world's leading musicians

TICKETS FOR SEPTEMBER– DECEMBER 2008 ON SALE NOW

Visit www.wigmore-hall.org.uk for full details and to book, or call the Box Office on 020 7935 2141.
For a free brochure email brochure@wigmore-hall.org.uk with your full postal address
(quoting 'BBC Proms') or call the Box Office.

To receive advance notice of all Wigmore Hall events, priority booking for Wigmore Series concerts,
10% off all Wigmore Hall Live CDs and many other benefits become a Friend of Wigmore Hall.
Visit www.wigmore-hall.org.uk/friends, email friends@wigmore-hall.org.uk or phone 020 7258 8230 for full details

Wigmore Hall, 36 Wigmore Street, London W1U 2BP. Director John Gilhooly Hon. FRAM
The Wigmore Hall Trust Registered Charity No. 1024838 www.wigmore-hall.org.uk Box Office: 020 7935 2141

PROMS PLUS

A new, expanded series of more than 70 introductions, interviews, workshops and other Proms-related events means that it is easier than ever to get to know the music and musicians featured during the season. **Clara Nissen** previews the Proms Plus series, while **Abigail Appleton** unveils the first Proms Literary Festival

The best things in life are free, they say, and this year's Proms Plus introductions are no exception. Free pre-Prom events have existed for years, but this season they've flourished into practically a festival in their own right: each day will bring at least one Proms Plus introduction, drawing on a wider range of formats and participants than ever before, in a fun and informative way. Every main evening concert will feature an associated event – all of which take place at the Royal College of Music's Britten Theatre, just across the road from the south side of the Royal Albert Hall. The series falls into a number of themed groups:

Proms Intro These comprise introductions of various forms – whether it's a conductor or soloist in conversation, a presentation from a musical expert, a round-table discussion or a showcase. Proms Intros are designed to leave you with a better understanding of the music you're about to hear, enhancing the concert experience. Highlights this season include conductor Sir Roger Norrington in conversation with BBC Rado 3 presenter Martin Handley before his concert with the SWR Symphony Orchestra Stuttgart; Pierre Boulez talking with Proms director Roger Wright before his all-Janáček Prom; and Emmanuelle Haïm in conversation with Suzy Klein on Monteverdi's *The Coronation of Poppea*, along with a specially made film based on the opera, made by young people.

Two Proms Intro events are dedicated exclusively to young composers: on 26 July the winners of last year's BBC Proms Inspire Young Composers' Competition showcase the latest fruits of their labours; and on 6 August you can hear pieces by the winners of this year's competition.

Music Intro (see also pages 60–67) Aimed at children aged 7-plus and their families, Music Intro workshops introduce the concert's music in an interactive and fun way. Bring along an instrument if you want to play along with the musicians, or just sit back and watch. Either way, you'll get a taster of the works you'll hear in the main evening Prom by playing or hearing excerpts of the music.

Proms Family Orchestra (see also pages 60–67) The Proms Family Orchestra gives everyone – whatever your age or ability – the chance to play alongside professional musicians. Sessions this year will explore the themes of folk, jazz and Doctor Who (alongside our first Doctor Who Prom).

Films This season's six Proms Films include celebrations three of the most important composer anniversaries of 2008 – those of Vaughan Williams, Messiaen and Stockhausen – including the 1948 film *Scott of the Antarctic* (for which Vaughan Williams wrote the soundtrack), taking you to the South Pole in time for Vaughan Williams's *Sinfonia antartica* later in the season. In a lighter vein, there are animal frolics in the BBC-commissioned animation of Janáček's opera *The Cunning Little Vixen* (see Listings for Proms 20, 40, 42, 50, 53 & 72).

Composer Portraits The Composer Portraits feature chamber music by four leading composers, each of whom will have a work premiered in the same day's Prom at the Royal Albert Hall. This year's composers are Simon Holt (25 July), Anders Hillborg

(13 August), Steven Stucky (28 August) and Mark-Anthony Turnage (8 September). Alongside performances by students from some of the UK's leading music conservatoires, and other young musicians, the composers will appear in conversation with a Radio 3 presenter. Composer Portraits are recorded by Radio 3 for broadcast later the same evening.

Proms Literary Festival New this year is the Proms Literary Festival, exploring themes of the Proms season, and the relationship between writers and composers (see page 72).

This year's Proms Plus events will be launched on the First Night of the Proms, with a special edition of Radio 3's *In Tune*, live from the Britten Theatre. Introducing the first Prom, and looking across the season, presenters Sean Rafferty and Petroc Trelawny will be talking to musicians appearing at the Proms, as well as previewing the Proms Literary Festival with poet and presenter Ian McMillan.

All Proms Plus events are free to ticket-holders for the following concert, and some are free to anyone (see Listings for details); many will be edited for broadcast on Radio 3 during concert intervals, and also available to listen to on the Proms website. And don't forget, if you're Promming in the Arena or Gallery, you can regain your place in the queue after the Proms Plus event (see page 53). ▶

Clara Nissen is Editorial Assistant, BBC Proms Publications

Proms Literary Festival

Music and literature have always been close bedfellows – whether you think of composers working with writers or drawing inspiration from literature, or writers finding a theme and a form in music. The Proms Literary Festival explores this relationship in different ways, but also offers a wider look at the literary and cultural world of which music is a part. Each event has been planned broadly to complement the concerts in this year's Proms season, but never simply to provide literary footnotes to the musical programmes.

From Rowan Williams, Stephen Poliakoff and Bridget Kendall on Russian writers to Claire Tomalin on Thomas Hardy and Christopher Ricks on A. E. Housman, the festival offers new readings of classics as well as – in the spirit of the Proms – a showcase for the work of contemporary writers, presenting a number of special commissions. Like the Proms, the Literary Festival will have performance at its heart, with readings of poetry and prose from leading actors. Most events will be broadcast, in edited form, on BBC Radio 3, and we hope the festival will have something to offer all types of Proms audiences, including families.

With the music of Ralph Vaughan Williams, alongside that of other English composers, threading through the season, the voices of English writers are a key theme in the Literary Festival. Music ran in Thomas Hardy's family and he played the violin with his father at local weddings. His love of music is evident both in the novels and in his moving and often very personal poetry, and critics have seen his early exposure to ballads as a significant influence on his verse. Hardy's work has in turn proved an inspiration to composers, in particular to Gerald Finzi. A passionate reader, Finzi also set words by William Wordsworth and on 19 July, before the performance of Finzi's *Intimations of Immortality*, biographer and critic Hermione Lee introduces a discussion of English Romanticism from Wordsworth to Hardy.

One of the pall-bearers at Thomas Hardy's funeral was A. E. Housman, author of *A Shropshire Lad*, and Housman is the focus of the literary event on 29 July, preceding George Butterworth's orchestral evocation of this enduring work. As well as taking a fresh look at *A Shropshire Lad*, Christopher Ricks, champion of Victorian poets and Professor of Poetry at Oxford University, will explore Housman's life and writing more widely.

All these writers, like so many English composers, were deeply engaged with the English countryside. Today the tradition of writing

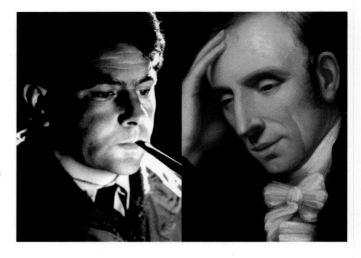

ABOVE
The Archbishop of Canterbury, Dr Rowan Williams, shares his thoughts on Dostoyevsky

ABOVE RIGHT
Composer Gerald Finzi (left), who set William Wordsworth (right) in his *Intimations of Immortality* for tenor, chorus and orchestra

on nature and the countryside is undergoing a revival in Britain, and the Literary Festival celebrates this in a number of events, including a look at one of the modern forms of pastoral, the way writers are finding inspiration in wildness and nature in cities (17 August).

Throughout the summer you can also enjoy literary journeys further afield – into space with poetry and prose inspired by the planets (10 September), and across oceans with writing about the sea (4 September). While, alongside some of this summer's Russian musical classics, the festival will offer four different approaches to Russian literary classics, including the Archbishop of Canterbury, Dr Rowan Williams, on Dostoyevsky (12 August) and television dramatist Stephen Poliakoff discussing his Russian literary passions (6 September).

Literary events are not new to the Proms – there have been *Poetry Proms* at the Serpentine Gallery and, more recently, two series of *The Adverb* at Cadogan Hall. Never before, though, have so many literary events been programmed alongside the concerts, nor presented, in the Royal College of Music's Britten Theatre, so close to the Royal Albert Hall and the epicentre of the Proms. ●

Abigail Appleton is Head of Speech Programming, BBC Radio 3

For details of all Proms Plus events, including Proms Literary Festival events, please see Listings, pages 92–127.

BBC SINGERS

Expand your musical horizons with the BBC Singers.
Visit **bbc.co.uk/singers** for details.

BBC RADIO

London Philharmonic Orchestra

Now on sale
2008/2009 Concert Season
at Southbank Centre's Royal Festival Hall

www.lpo.org.uk
full details online

Call 020 7840 4242
**Mon-Fri 10am – 5pm for a free
season brochure**

Opening concert
Wednesday 24 September 2008 | 7.30pm
Royal Festival Hall

Vaughan Williams *Symphony 8*
Turnage *Mambo, Blues and Tarantella*
— Violin Concerto (world première)
Ligeti *Atmosphères*
Stravinsky *The Rite of Spring*

Vladimir Jurowski *conductor*
Christian Tetzlaff *violin*

RESIDENT AT
**SOUTHBANK
CENTRE**

THE PROMS – WHEREVER YOU ARE

With extensive coverage on BBC Radio 3, Television and Online, it's easier than ever to get access to the Proms. **Graeme Kay** talks to BBC staff who play a key role in bringing the Proms to you

BBC RADIO 3

90 – 93FM

The Proms on BBC Radio 3

- Every Prom live on Radio 3 (90–93FM)
- Many Proms repeats during *Afternoon on 3* (weekdays, 2.00pm), plus a series of repeats over the Christmas period
- Special edition of *In Tune* to launch the season (Friday 18 July, 5.00pm)
- *Summer CD Review* with Andrew McGregor – presenting CD releases of artists and repertoire featuring at the Proms

Brian Jackson *Senior Producer, Radio 3 (with responsibility for the Proms)*

"I've been producing individual Proms for nine years, and 2008 will be my third year overseeing the whole season. My job is to make sure that the radio broadcasts run smoothly.

A typical day might involve a 10.00am rehearsal for a Proms Chamber Music concert at Cadogan Hall, making sure that the artists, presenters and production team have what they need. Then it's down to the Royal Albert Hall for the rehearsal for the evening Prom; I'll discuss the sound-balance with our engineers, arrange an interview with a performer, or I might have to sort out an administrative problem. During the rehearsal the presenter works on their script, which changes constantly, even right up to the concert: the presenter will often pick up interesting details and impressions during rehearsals, and a conductor or soloist may come up with an insightful comment that we can weave into our presentation.

Between the rehearsal and concert we always have a production meeting, when we go over all the details of timings and stage-management; it involves representatives from the orchestra, the Proms team, Radio 3, Television (if the concert's being screened) and the Hall. The aim is to dovetail what happens on the stage with what happens on the airwaves so it all runs seamlessly. The cardinal sin is if the broadcast holds up the concert on the stage! Despite our best efforts, this does happen occasionally. But mostly the cause is something backstage – a missing player, a lost piece of music, or something totally unexpected – like when a conductor one night took a phone call seconds before he was due to follow the orchestra's Leader on to the stage. The hall went silent, but we couldn't do that on radio; that's when preparation, experience and a presenter's talent for ad-libbing kicks in!

The hub of our activity takes place in our backstage production office. Here we record interviews with artists, presenters tap away at computers, sound engineers prepare mixing-desks and producers pace up and down checking their timings. During the concert itself the room doubles as a mixing studio from where the BBC World Service production team runs its broadcasts. It can all get a bit cramped, especially on days with two Proms – but it does engender a strong sense of camaraderie.

During each Prom, the microphone feeds are mixed down to a final stereo balance by a team of sound engineers in a large truck (called a DSV – Digital Sound Vehicle) outside Door 11; the mix is beamed from there to Broadcasting House and then transmitted around the world. On radio we're trying to achieve a balance that I'd describe as 'the best seat in the house'; our engineers are expert at bringing out all the musical detail while making sure you can 'hear' the hall – conveying that unique quality that tells the listener this could only be a performance from the Royal Albert Hall.

Fourteen producers work on the Proms (including those attached year-round to individual BBC performing groups), as well as a small team of Broadcast Assistants, and of course we also work

on Radio 3's non-Proms programmes. For all of us there is a real sense of pride and achievement in bringing such a fantastic series of concerts to radio listeners – from the opening chord of the First Night, right through to the final cheer of the Last. There's a great excitement in entering the Royal Albert Hall for the first time each season and seeing it fully rigged for broadcasts, and it would be all too easy to spend seven days a week at the Proms.

My survival tip is to pace yourself, and not to go to everything throughout the summer. It's a long season, and some nights you too should enjoy 'the best seat in the house' from the comfort of your own home." ●

A CROWD OF POSSIBILITIES ON RADIO 3

'We never stop thinking about the Proms,' says Edward Blakeman, Editor for Radio 3's Proms coverage, 'about what might be different, what new features we might bring to it. The Proms lasts for two months, then you're only 10 months away from the next season, which in planning terms is not a vast amount of time. And there's always a welcome reminder after each season, because our Proms repeats are an important part of Radio 3's festivities during the Christmas period.'

While Radio 3's core offering for the Proms remains immutable – every concert is broadcast live – there is always scope to enhance the listening experience with associated programming such as interval talks, features on *Music Matters*, previews in *Breakfast* and artist interviews on *In Tune*. New for 2008 is a rethink of some of the concert intervals. Over the years the Proms has steadily increased the number and variety of its introductory events – for example Composer Portrait concerts. This year, a number of events from the new Proms Plus series – talks, interviews and panel discussions – will be recorded and edited for broadcast on Radio 3 during the interval of the immediately following concert.

'There are technical challenges in this,' admits Blakeman, 'because of pressure on editing time between the Proms Plus event and the start of the interval. But the result will be to build a stronger, more vivid connection between the listening audience at home and around the world, and the excitement of the live experience. On Radio 3 we always want to take you to more than just the concert!'

The Proms on BBC Television

- New weekly Saturday-night Proms on BBC Two
- Regular coverage on BBC Four
- Background notes via the red button for televised concerts (on satellite, cable and Freeview)
- High Definition and 5.1 surround sound for broadcasts on the BBC's High Definition service, BBC HD
- Take your seat for the Last Night of the Proms (first half on BBC Two and second half on BBC One) – plus Proms in the Park coverage from around the UK

Oliver Macfarlane *Editor, BBC Classical Music Television*
(Series Editor, Proms)

"The Proms season is the 'jewel in the crown' of BBC Classical Music Television's output. It's the most intense period of live and recorded music production in our calendar, and of course it culminates in a spectacular media event: the Last Night. We broadcast the Proms on four of the BBC channels: BBC One, BBC Two and BBC Four, as well as some High Definition broadcasts in 5.1 surround sound on BBC HD.

With the growth of the Proms in the Park events, we have been able to broadcast from around the country, reflecting the Proms as a truly national activity. British people have always enjoyed the opportunity to sing along in a massive group, whether it's belting out football chants, rugby anthems or the traditional songs of the Last Night. And, by bringing the Proms in the Park events into the Last Night festivities at the Royal Albert Hall, we've been able to bring music-making from around the UK into the overall experience. I'm sure Henry Wood would have approved!

At the Royal Albert Hall the most obvious sign of our presence – apart from the cameras in the hall, which we try to make as discreet as possible – is the small gathering of BBC trucks (they're often called 'scanners') that you can see outside the hall. These stay put throughout the season, but we pull the cameras out when they're not being used.

This year BBC Four will continue last season's pattern of coverage, with Proms broadcasts spread throughout the season. In previous years we've clumped concerts into mini seasons but I think the public prefers to have regular appointments to view, rather than a less regular schedule of feast or famine. The BBC Two offering will also be extended, featuring not only a regular Saturday-evening slot, but a series of 'best of' broadcasts.

"With the growth of the Proms in the Park events, we have been able to broadcast from around the country, reflecting the Proms as a truly national activity."

It's very gratifying when viewers who so obviously appreciate the broadcasts call for every Prom to be televised! Much as we'd like to do that, of course, you can't escape the economics: we're investing just as much in the Proms but, in spite of the economies of scale, there is still a heavy additional cost in putting extra concerts into the schedule. But it's worth remembering that ten years ago only a handful of Proms were televised!

I'm very much looking forward to the 2008 season. I think that in the television coverage we'll be playing our part in reflecting the broad artistic scope of the Proms – with the inclusion this year of Late Night performances and world music – reflecting the approach of Radio 3." ●

IN THE COMPANY OF BBC TWO

This year BBC Two is extending its Proms coverage. 'There will be live concerts, including the First Night, as always,' says Television Series Editor Oliver Macfarlane, 'but we're introducing some "best of" programmes, which will include parts of more than one Prom. Compiling material from several concerts means that our viewers will be able to catch a greater number of performances. And we'll also be able to include performances from Late Night concerts, which haven't previously been screened, since their timings don't fit comfortably into the broadcast schedule. Furthermore, the fact that edited concerts don't have intervals adds up to more music on screen!'

Featured among the 'best of' concerts will be a Nigel Kennedy special (on 26 July) comprising Elgar's Violin Concerto conducted by Vernon Handley, and a Late Night performance with the Nigel Kennedy Quintet (Proms 2 & 3). On 9 August a live broadcast of jazz-inspired orchestral music under Charles Hazlewood (Prom 31), includes a recorded excerpt from a Late Night Prom given by the King's Singers earlier that week (Prom 26). And a 'Great Conductors' programme on 16 August brings together Daniel Barenboim with his West-Eastern Divan Orchestra (Prom 38) and Pierre Boulez conducting the BBC Symphony Orchestra (Prom 40).

Roger Philbrick *Senior Content Producer, BBC Audio and Music Interactive (with responsibility for bbc.co.uk/proms)*

"I'm an amateur musician with a background in science and broadcast engineering, so this job is a delight: it allows me to indulge my passions for music and technology. Trying to offer consistently high-quality content over a range of constantly evolving platforms (*eg* Internet, mobile phones, interactive television) is quite a challenge.

In February we start setting up the Proms website, working with designers and technical colleagues to create a fresh look and incorporate new features, such as the excellent BBC iPlayer, which will deliver all 2008 Proms broadcasts. We reflect the efforts of many other teams and individuals, so I spend much of my time liaising with producers and contributors as well as co-ordinating the website staff.

We aim to provide a huge amount of information in an accessible form. Whether you're interested in composers, performers, talks or family events, we want to make it easy to find relevant details and to highlight other music or artists that you might like to hear. We want to offer a seamless one-stop online shop, taking you from finding out about the music to arranging a visit to the Royal Albert Hall, finding out the Proms in the Park locations, or helping you to plan your listening and viewing on BBC Radio 3 and Television.

BBC Online highlights
– bbc.co.uk/proms

- Full listings on the Proms web and WAP sites
- Check concert details via your mobile phone
- Easy access to the latest Proms iPlayer, providing radio and television content throughout the season
- Full programme notes for each of the works, available on the website
- Send us your reviews and find out what others thought
- Celebrate the Last Night at Proms in the Park events all over the UK
- Daily text alerts to keep you up-to-date with each day's concerts and events

From spring until the end of the season we're in constant contact with the Proms editorial and marketing teams, adding topical information and ensuring that any changes of artist, works or broadcast times are quickly reflected on the website. And from the First Night onwards we update the site several times each day – so we have to make sure we have the staff in place at a time when many people are on holiday.

By the time each Prom broadcast begins, we will have published the full programme notes online for the concert; and we then look forward to posting visitors' reviews of the performances – whether they've enjoyed them or not! Interaction with our users

"It's a non-stop white-knuckle ride until the final bars of 'Auld Lang Syne' at the Last Night. Then I take a well-earned holiday."

is central to the website; last year we launched a new 'Prommers' World' section and we encourage comments on Radio 3's Performance messageboard. Facebook and MySpace members will find that the BBC Proms has a presence there too.

The concerts are all streamed live via the website, and when they're over, the new BBC iPlayer offers access to the radio and television broadcasts for another seven days.

People on the move can get the latest Proms information via mobile phone – full listings are carried on our dedicated WAP site; and the text club offers daily updates for each day's concerts.

New for the Proms this year is Proms Plus, an expanded programme of pre-concert events (see page 70–72), including Music Intro sessions to which you can bring your family to meet the musicians and learn about the music they'll be playing. These events will also be reflected on the website.

The Proms site is hugely rewarding to work on. It's a non-stop white-knuckle ride until the final bars of 'Auld Lang Syne' at the Last Night. Then, during September – in common with many Proms colleagues – I take a well-earned holiday. And I'm not long back before we start thinking about the following year's website." ●

Graeme Kay is an Interactive Producer for BBC Audio and Music, and former Editor of BBC Music Magazine.

THE ONE-STOP ONLINE SHOP

'The Proms website is one of the most-visited sites on www.bbc.co.uk,' says Roland Taylor, Interactive Editor with responsibility for the Proms, Radio 3 and Classical Music TV. 'It comes into its own during the Proms season itself, of course, but it remains an important resource throughout the year to keep users informed with news about the plans, about booking, and about the music itself.'

The BBC's most important and popular interactive innovation of the last few years has been the ability to 'listen again' to radio programmes, over the Internet, during a seven-day window after broadcast. 'This – and the growing roster of podcasts available from BBC sites – has given listeners the opportunity in effect to determine their own listening schedule,' says Taylor. 'This year, radio and television have been combined in a new service – the iPlayer – which means that Proms audiences will be able to watch as well as listen again to broadcast concerts. Through new media technology such as the iPlayer even more people can be part of the Proms experience.'

Chris Christodoulou (p80 bottom right)

BBC SCOTTISH SYMPHONY ORCHESTRA

ILAN VOLKOV, CHIEF CONDUCTOR
DONALD RUNNICLES, CHIEF CONDUCTOR ELECT
STEFAN SOLYOM, ASSOCIATE GUEST CONDUCTOR

BBC PROMS SEASON 2008 INCLUDES

Ilan Volkov conducts the world premiere of **Jonathan Harvey's** Speakings
Donald Runnicles conducts Mahler Das Lied von der Erde
Stefan Solyom conducts Ethel Smyth Concerto for violin, horn and orchestra

EDINBURGH INTERNATIONAL FESTIVAL 2008

Ilan Volkov conducts Messiaen Éclairs sur l'au-delà
Gennadi Rozhdestvensky conducts Tippett A Child of our Time

GLASGOW CONCERT SEASON 2008/09

Celebrating **Stravinsky** and **Rachmaninov**, including the complete cycle of piano concertos.

ABERDEEN CONCERT SEASON 2008/09

Featuring American music, including works by **Carter**, **Copland**, **Bernstein** and **Gershwin**

"WHAT A REMARKABLE OUTFIT THE BAND HAS BECOME, THE BBC SCOTTISH SYMPHONY ORCHESTRA IS FIRING ON ALL CYLINDERS" THE OBSERVER

BBC.CO.UK/BBCSSO

BBC SCOTLAND, CITY HALLS, CANDLERIGGS, GLASGOW G1 1NQ

90 – 93 FM

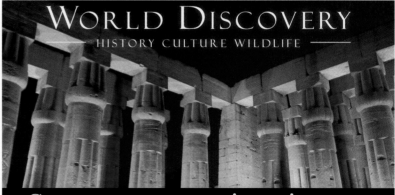

Classic Radio

PURE EVOKE-1S
Now playing...

EVOKE-1S
Luxury portable DAB digital and FM radio

PURE EVOKE-1S
January 08

01923 277488
www.pure.com

EcoPlus

digital radio

Designed in the UK

THE QUEEN'S AWARDS
FOR ENTERPRISE:
INNOVATION
2004

PURE
World leaders in DAB digital radio

Photo: Simón Bolívar Youth Orchestra of Venezuela, Gustavo Dudamel, Music Director © Jennifer Taylor/New York Times/Eyevine

SOUTHBANK CENTRE

SHELL CLASSIC INTERNATIONAL 2008/09

GREAT ORCHESTRAS FROM AROUND THE WORLD AT ROYAL FESTIVAL HALL

WEDNESDAY 1 OCTOBER 2008
BUDAPEST FESTIVAL ORCHESTRA
Iván Fischer *conductor*

Schoenberg Verklärte Nacht;
Mahler Das Lied von der Erde

SATURDAY 4 OCTOBER 2008
ORCHESTRE REVOLUTIONNAIRE ET ROMANTIQUE MONTEVERDI CHOIR
John Eliot Gardiner *conductor*

A selection of Brahms' favourite *a capella* folksong settings;
Brahms Songs for mixed a capella choir, Op.104;
Symphony No.3

SUNDAY 5 OCTOBER 2008
ORCHESTRE REVOLUTIONNAIRE ET ROMANTIQUE MONTEVERDI CHOIR
John Eliot Gardiner *conductor*

A selection of motets, psalms and cantata choruses by Heinrich Schütz and JS Bach; **Brahms** Fest-und Gedenksprüche, Op.109; Symphony No.4

MONDAY 24 NOVEMBER 2008
CHAMBER ORCHESTRA OF EUROPE
Mitsuko Uchida *piano/director*
Alexander Janiček *director*

Stravinsky Apollon musagéte;
Mozart Piano Concerto No.23 in A, K.488; Piano Concerto No.24 in C minor, K.491

SATURDAY 29 NOVEMBER 2008
BAVARIAN RADIO SYMPHONY ORCHESTRA
Mariss Jansons *conductor*

Mozart Symphony No.36 (Linz);
Bruckner Symphony No.4 (Romantic)

WEDNESDAY 10 DECEMBER 2008
ENSEMBLE INTERCONTEMPORAIN
Pierre Boulez *conductor*
Pierre-Laurent Aimard *piano*

Messiaen Couleurs de la Cité Céleste; Sept Haïkaï;
Boulez sur Incises

THURSDAY 11 DECEMBER 2008
ENSEMBLE INTERCONTEMPORAIN
Pierre Boulez *conductor*
Pierre-Laurent Aimard *piano*

Carter Clarinet Concerto; Dialogues; Caténaires, for solo piano; **Boulez** Derive II
Queen Elizabeth Hall

THURSDAY 19 FEBRUARY 2009
VIENNA PHILHARMONIC ORCHESTRA
Zubin Mehta *conductor*

Haydn Symphony No.104 (London); **Bruckner** Symphony No.9

SUNDAY 29 MARCH 2009
BAVARIAN RADIO SYMPHONY ORCHESTRA
Mariss Jansons *conductor*

Beethoven Symphony No.3 (Eroica); **Strauss** Four Last Songs; **Ravel** Daphnis et Chloé – Suite No.2

TUESDAY 14 &
SATURDAY 18 APRIL 2009
SIMON BOLIVAR YOUTH ORCHESTRA OF VENEZUELA
Gustavo Dudamel *music director*

Programmes include:
Bartók Concerto for Orchestra (Tuesday 14 April); **Stravinsky** The Rite of Spring (Saturday 18 April)

TUESDAY 21 APRIL 2009
CHAMBER ORCHESTRA OF EUROPE
Pierre-Laurent Aimard *piano/director*

Beethoven Piano Concerto No.1; Piano Concerto No.2; Piano Concerto No.3

SUNDAY 17 MAY 2009
ZURICH OPERA ORCHESTRA LA SCINTILLA
Marc Minkowski *conductor*

Handel Agrippina

FRIDAY 29 MAY 2009
CHAMBER ORCHESTRA OF ORCHESTRA
Yuri Temirkanov *conductor*
Denis Matsuev *piano*

Prokofiev Symphony No.1 in D (Classical); **Shostakovich** Concerto No.1 for piano, trumpet & strings; **Debussy** Prélude à l'après-midi d'un faune; **Bizet** Symphony in C

Tickets from £65 - £9

Shell Classic International: Part of Shell's major sponsorship of the Transformation of Southbank Centre's Royal Festival Hall.

TICKETS 0871 663 2503
WWW.SOUTHBANKCENTRE.CO.UK

ARTS COUNCIL ENGLAND

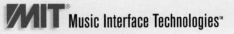

PIERINO
PASTA PIZZA RESTAURANT

Telephone 020 7581 3770

Monday to Friday 12–3.00pm, 5.30–11.30pm

Saturday & Sunday 12 noon–11.30pm

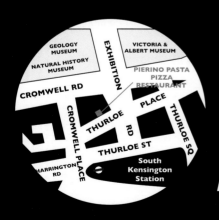

Prompt service guaranteed for you to be in time for the performance.

We are within walking distance of the Royal Albert Hall, near South Kensington tube station.

You are welcome before and after the performance.

EXPERIENCE OF SERVING GENUINE ITALIAN FOOD AND FOR
HOME-MADE PASTA AND THE BEST PIZZA IN LONDON

30 YEARS

CONCERT LISTINGS

ADVANCE BOOKING

By post and online *from Monday 21 April*

GENERAL BOOKING

In person, by phone or online *from Tuesday 27 May*

Telephone: 0845 401 5040*
Online: bbc.co.uk/proms

For full booking information and Advance Booking Form see *pages 130–144*

PRICE CODES

A ▾ G Each concert falls into one of seven price bands, colour-coded for ease of reference.
For full list of prices see *page 139*
For special offers see *page 136*

NB: concert start-times vary across the season – check before you book

All concert details were correct at the time of going to press. The BBC reserves the right to alter artist or programme details as necessary.

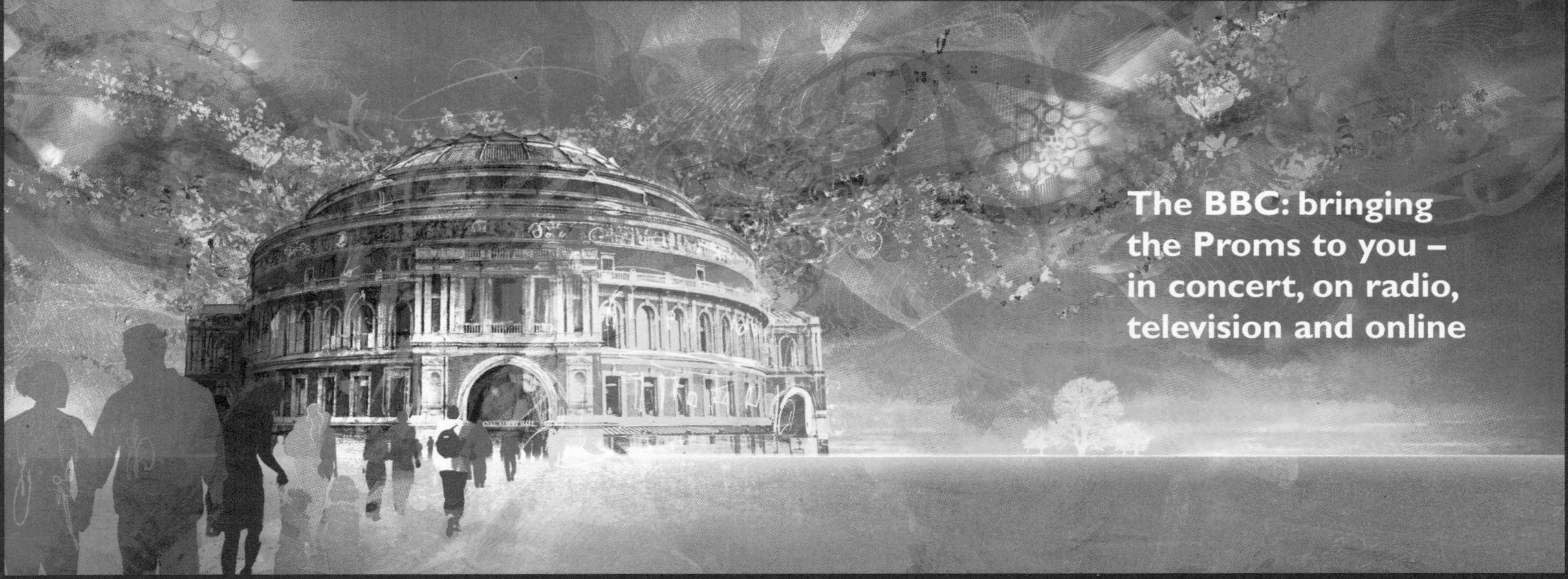

The BBC: bringing the Proms to you – in concert, on radio, television and online

**Calls from a BT landline are charged at local rate. Charges from mobiles and other networks may be higher*

WEEKEND PROMMING PASS – BEAT THE QUEUES AND SAVE MONEY (SEE PAGE 136)

PROM 1

FRIDAY 18 JULY

Proms Plus 5.00pm, Royal College of Music
In Tune Sean Rafferty and Petroc Trelawny present a special edition of *In Tune*, live from the RCM, featuring Proms artists, live music and a preview of the Proms Literary Festival with Ian McMillan.
Free to all. Tickets available from 27 May – please phone 0870 901 1227

8.00pm–c10.25pm, Royal Albert Hall

R. Strauss
Festliches Präludium   *12'*

Mozart
Oboe Concerto in C major, K314   *20'*

R. Strauss
Four Last Songs   *22'*

interval

Messiaen
La Nativité du Seigneur – Dieu parmi nous   *8'*

Beethoven
Rondo in B flat major for piano and orchestra   *10'*

Elliott Carter
Caténaires for solo piano   *4'*
UK premiere

Scriabin
The Poem of Ecstasy   *20'*

Karita Mattila *soprano*
Pierre-Laurent Aimard *piano*
Nicholas Daniel *oboe*
Wayne Marshall *organ*

Royal College of Music Brass
BBC Symphony Orchestra
Jiří Bělohlávek *conductor*

The opening Prom launches our centenary celebrations of Elliott Carter and Olivier Messiaen, and features three soloists who will make return visits during the season. See 'The Light of Sound', pages 20–25; 'Modernism with Soul', pages 38–39; 'New Music', pages 42–49

Broadcast
RADIO Live on Radio 3
ONLINE Live and 'listen again' options at bbc.co.uk/proms
TV Live on BBC Two

PROM 2

SATURDAY 19 JULY

Proms Plus 4.45pm, Royal College of Music
Proms Literary Festival Hermione Lee discusses English Romanticism from William Wordsworth to Thomas Hardy with Hardy's biographer Claire Tomalin, Duncan Wu and Kate Kennedy.
Free to ticket-holders. Edited broadcast on Radio 3 later this evening

6.30pm–c9.00pm, Royal Albert Hall

Bax
The Garden of Fand   *17'*

Finzi
Intimations of Immortality   *43'*

interval

Elgar
Violin Concerto   *52'*

Andrew Kennedy *tenor*
Nigel Kennedy *violin*

BBC Symphony Chorus
BBC Concert Orchestra
Vernon Handley *conductor*

Nigel Kennedy

Maverick violinist Nigel Kennedy returns to the Proms – after an absence of 21 years – for Elgar's Violin Concerto, the work that first put him on the musical map following his now-classic recording of it under tonight's conductor. With Vernon Handley in charge, this programme of British music is in good hands: few other conductors bring such a wealth of experience to the music of Bax – *The Garden of Fand* mines deep seams of late-Romanticism. And another Kennedy – Andrew (no relation, who appeared at the Proms as recently as last year's Last Night) – brings us Gerald Finzi's touching setting of Wordsworth, a study of the loss of childhood innocence.

SAME-DAY SAVER Book for both Proms 2 and 3 and save (see page 136)

Broadcast
RADIO Live on Radio 3
ONLINE Live and 'listen again' options at bbc.co.uk/proms
TV Elgar recorded for broadcast on BBC Two on 26 July.

PROM 3

SATURDAY 19 JULY

10.00pm–c11.30pm, Royal Albert Hall

NKQ – Nigel Kennedy Quintet

Nigel Kennedy *electric violin*
Tomasz Grzegorski *saxophones*
Piotr Wyleżol *piano*
Adam Kowalewski *double bass/electric bass*
Paweł Dobrowolski *percussion*

with

Xantone Blacq *singer*

'People can say I'm a classical violinist if they want to, but I've always viewed myself as a musician who plays music and not just a certain part of it.' Tonight's second Prom offers an opportunity to judge Nigel Kennedy's comment for yourself. For the past few years Kennedy has been living in Poland, exploring the country's rich musical heritage – and he has also been teaming up with some of Poland's finest jazz musicians, the fruits of which you can hear tonight.

There will be no interval

Nigel Kennedy Quintet

Broadcast
RADIO Live on Radio 3
ONLINE Live and 'listen again' options at bbc.co.uk/proms
TV Recorded for broadcast on BBC Two on 26 July

Folk Day

Bellowhead

From the deep-rooted influence on Vaughan Williams's music to the ongoing rise of young British folk musicians, this year's Proms Folk Day offers the chance to immerse yourself in music, dance and storytelling. With its ability to characterise a community, folk music offers a unique reflection of different cultures and traditions. Many composers across the centuries have taken inspiration from folk tunes, drawing their colourful scales and vigorous rhythms into the world of Western classical music.

In a day featuring a range of free activities, there's a special, *free* Prom in the afternoon (Prom 4). With performances from The Sage Gateshead's ground-breaking Folkestra, Hungarian folk musicians Muzsikás, the London Sinfonietta and young musicians from London, this concert celebrates the living tradition, the folk influence on great composers (Grainger, Vaughan Williams, Berio and Bartók) and some new collaborations in a finale involving all performers.

In the evening concert (Prom 5) we showcase some of the UK's most exciting folk talent. The day ends the only way a Folk Day should, with a riotous ceilidh in the Royal Albert Hall Arena. See 'All Together Now …', pages 60–67. For details of free events throughout the day, including workshops with the Proms Folk Family Choir and Orchestra, and an afternoon mini folk festival, see page 61, or visit bbc.co.k/proms

SUNDAY 20 JULY – FOLK DAY

Proms Plus Royal College of Music (except 12.00noon)
10.00am Proms Folk Family Orchestra Come and join us to create a folk-inspired premiere (see page 67).
10.00am Proms Folk Family Chorus The chance to learn folk songs from around the British Isles (see page 67).
12noon Proms Folk in the Park Mini folk festival (Kensington Gardens, see page 61)
Free to all.

3.30pm–c6.00pm, Royal Albert Hall

*This is a **free** event. Tickets will be available from the Royal Albert Hall Box Office (in person, online at bbc.co.uk/proms or by phone – 0845 401 5040) from Monday 30 June. (Season Tickets, Half-Season Tickets and Weekend Promming Passes will be valid for this event.)*

Traditional folk songs*

Folk-song-inspired works by
Grainger and **Vaughan Williams**   15'

Berio
Folk Songs   25'

Trad., arr. Folkestra
Folk music from the British Isles

Folk music from Transylvania, the Eastern Carpathian Mountains and Moldova   15'

Bartók
Romanian Dances   13'
interspersed with traditional folk-song settings

Kathryn Tickell
New arrangement   c8'
BBC commission: world premiere

Bella Hardy* singer
London Young Musicians
Folkestra
Muzsikás
London Sinfonietta
Martyn Brabbins conductor

There will be one interval

Broadcast
RADIO Live on Radio 3
ONLINE Live and 'listen again' options at bbc.co.uk/proms

Proms Plus 5.45pm, Royal College of Music
Proms Literary Festival Ian McMillan and his Orchestra present a cabaret of words and music, showcasing the connections between folk music, poetry and storytelling. **Free to all.** Edited broadcast on Radio 3 during tonight's interval

7.30pm–c9.30pm, Royal Albert Hall

To include sets by:
Bella Hardy singer
Martin Simpson singer/guitar
Bellowhead

There will be one interval

Martin Simpson

Following the free afternoon concert exploring how folk music has influenced classical composers, Proms Folk Day's evening concert focuses on artists who are continuing, reviving and reinterpreting the traditions of English folk music. Tonight's Prom presents a fascinating picture of the many directions folk music is taking, and includes appearances from Derbyshire-born singer Bella Hardy, guitarist Martin Simpson and the boisterous 11-piece big band Bellowhead – winners of three Radio 2 Folk Awards.

Broadcast
RADIO Live on Radio 3
ONLINE Live and 'listen again' options at bbc.co.uk/proms
TV Live on BBC Four

10.00pm–c10.45pm, Royal Albert Hall Arena

Ceilidh

Join your partners in the Arena, or just watch from your seat, as the London Lasses and Pete Quinn lead the dancing in an energetic final flourish to Proms Folk Day. *Free to ticket-holders for the 7.30pm concert; dancers require a free dancing ticket, available from Tuesday 27 May by calling the Box Office 0845 401 5040.*

MONDAY 21 JULY

1.00pm–c2.00pm

Proms Chamber Music at Cadogan Hall

Schumann
Gesänge der Frühe, Op. 133   *12'*

Elliott Carter
Night Fantasies   *21'*

Messiaen
Catalogue d'oiseaux – L'alouette lulu   *9'*

Bartók
Out of Doors – suite   *12'*

Pierre-Laurent Aimard *piano*

A programme typical of the ever-questing Pierre-Laurent Aimard, blending music from different periods. Schumann's last piano work looks forward with its harmonically advanced language. Its mood is taken up by Elliott Carter's classic *Night Fantasies* of 1980, a work described by its composer as 'a piano piece of continuously changing moods, suggesting the fleeting thoughts and feelings that pass through the mind during a period of wakefulness at night'. The ever modern-sounding Bartók is represented by his *Out of Doors* suite, written very much with himself in mind as performer. It exploits the piano's percussive qualities to winning effect. And as a leading exponent of Messiaen's piano music, Aimard offers a sketch of a night bird, 'L'alouette lulu' (The Woodlark). *See 'The Light of Sound', pages 20–25; 'Modernism with Soul', pages 38–39*

There will be no interval

Broadcast
RADIO Live on Radio 3
ONLINE Live and 'listen again' options at bbc.co.uk/proms

Spotlight on …
Pierre-Laurent Aimard

As well as giving the UK premiere of Elliott Carter's fast-moving *Caténaires* (Prom 1) and taking the solo-piano role in Messiaen's *Turangalîla Symphony* (Prom 64), Pierre-Laurent Aimard combines these two composers with Schumann and Bartók in his Proms Chamber Music recital. Aimard first met Carter over 30 years ago, while learning some of his chamber music, 'but in recent years I've been playing more and more of his music'.

Aimard's connection with Messiaen stems from earlier still: as a 12-year-old student at the Paris Conservatoire, his teacher was Yvonne Loriod, Messiaen's wife and muse, through whom he met the composer. 'Messiaen was a very peaceful, sweet and passionate man,' Aimard recalls, 'with a great aural ability and a huge energy for working. The fact that his music makes so much sense to so many people around the world shows that it goes beyond the confines of being described in terms of religion alone.'

MONDAY 21 JULY

Proms Plus 5.45pm, Royal College of Music
Proms Intro Olivier Latry – who performs Messiaen in the evening Prom, talks to Tom Service about the great French composer.
Free to ticket-holders. Edited broadcast on Radio 3 during tonight's interval

7.30pm–c9.45pm, Royal Albert Hall

Messiaen
L'Ascension (for organ)   *24'*

Et exspecto resurrectionem mortuorum   *31'*

interval

Saint-Saëns
Symphony No. 3, 'Organ'   *36'*

Olivier Latry *organ*

Orchestre Philharmonique de Radio France
Myung-Whun Chung *conductor*

A double opportunity to celebrate Olivier Messiaen's instrument, the organ. Olivier Latry, who teaches at the Paris Conservatoire (as did Messiaen), presents two faces of the French organ tradition – solo Messiaen and Saint-Saëns's much-loved 'Organ' Symphony, a work written for London. (Latry's recent recording of the work was a 'Building a Library' choice on Radio 3's *CD Review*.) Between the two organ works comes Messiaen's *Et exspecto resurrectionem mortuorum*, a magnificent memorial to the dead of two world wars, and a haunting exploration of instrumental colour. A leading interpreter of Messiaen's music, tonight's conductor took part in the first performance of Messiaen's posthumously completed *Concert à quatre* (Prom 45), of which he is the dedicatee. *See 'The Light of Sound', pages 20–25*

Broadcast
RADIO Live on Radio 3
ONLINE Live and 'listen again' options at bbc.co.uk/proms
TV Live on BBC Four

TUESDAY 22 JULY

Proms Plus 5.15pm, Royal College of Music
Proms Intro Sir Roger Norrington, one of today's most versatile conductors, talks to Martin Handley about the challenge of working with different orchestras.
Free to ticket-holders. Edited broadcast on Radio 3 during tonight's interval

7.00pm–c9.05pm, Royal Albert Hall

Rossini
William Tell – Overture   *12'*

Haydn
Cello Concerto No. 1 in C major   *24'*

interval

Elgar
Symphony No. 1 in A flat major   *50'*

Jean-Guihen Queyras *cello*

Stuttgart Radio Symphony Orchestra (SWR)
Sir Roger Norrington *conductor*

Sir Roger Norrington

Rossini's *William Tell* Overture opens the programme, and its long cello solo sets the scene for Haydn's C major Cello Concerto, which features French cellist Jean-Guihen Queyras in his Proms debut. Norrington and his German orchestra also perform the work with which Elgar began to win acclaim as a symphonist in Germany as well as in England.

Broadcast
RADIO Live on Radio 3
ONLINE Live and 'listen again' options at bbc.co.uk/proms

TUESDAY 22 JULY

10.00pm–c11.30pm, Royal Albert Hall

Obrecht
Missa 'Malheur me bat'   *40'*

Josquin des Prez
Missa 'Malheur me bat'   *40'*

Tallis Scholars
Peter Phillips *conductor*

The Tallis Scholars and conductor Peter Phillips have established themselves as one of the UK's finest interpreters of Renaissance polyphonic music. In this Late Night Prom they explore two 15th-century Masses based on the chanson 'Malheur me bat' (Misfortune has struck me), attributed to Jean de Ockeghem. The Flemish Jacob Obrecht – the 550th anniversary of whose birth we celebrate this year – was highly regarded in his day, eclipsed only by Josquin des Prez. Josquin's 'Malheur me bat' setting captures something of the sorrow of Josquin's patron Cardinal Ascanio Sforza, who had been exiled from Milan, taking Josquin with him. The programme also includes a performance of the original, three-part 'Malheur me bat' song, with specially commissioned words.

There will be no interval

Broadcast
RADIO Live on Radio 3
ONLINE Live and 'listen again' options at bbc.co.uk/proms

Spotlight on ... Peter Phillips

"My earliest memory of Renaissance polyphony was at school, when the chapel choir sang 'O clap your hands' by Orlando Gibbons. I couldn't believe how involved, yet artless, it was.

Unlike the revival of other early music in the 1970s, Renaissance polyphony like these Masses is a continuing tradition: our cathedral choirs have sung them immemorially. However, the 15th-century chanson 'Malheur me bat', which is probably by Jean de Ockeghem, hasn't been sung for centuries in its original form because the words have been lost.

These two Masses by Obrecht and Josquin both use the melody of 'Malheur me bat'. Obrecht quotes the melody so you can hear it in undecorated form, and it just sits there in one voice throughout the Mass: you can hear it quite clearly. Josquin had a way with mathematical music that was second to none, and he breaks up the melody and uses it in very clever ways. The last movement works the melody into a canon – it really is the crowning of the whole Mass."

SAME-DAY SAVER Book for both Proms 7 and 8 and save (see page 136)

Tallis Scholars

WEDNESDAY 23 JULY ✗

Proms Plus 5.15pm, Royal College of Music
Proms Literary Festival Matthew Sweet profiles the cultural events of 1958, with writers Alan Sillitoe, Diana Athill and Anthony Thwaite, and historian Dominic Sandbrook.
Free to ticket-holders. Edited broadcast on Radio 3 later this evening

7.00pm–c10.05pm, Royal Albert Hall

Mendelssohn
Overture 'Ruy Blas' *8'*

Symphony No. 4 in A major, 'Italian' *28'*

interval

Brahms
Piano Concerto No. 2 in B flat major *48'*

interval

Brahms
Symphony No. 2 in D major *40'*

Lars Vogt *piano*

BBC Symphony Orchestra
Jiří Bělohlávek *conductor*

A Proms reprise of a programme first given in 1958, featuring two German composers who managed to retain Classical poise in the face of burgeoning Romanticism. Mendelssohn's Fourth Symphony celebrates the sounds and colours of Italy, while Brahms's Second is the most 'pastoral' of his symphonies, a work of carefree high spirits. In between comes the colossal Second Piano Concerto with which Brahms blurs the boundaries between symhony and concerto; the soloist is Lars Vogt, whose reputation is similarly built on a mastery of the Classical repertoire. Mendelssohn's spirited curtain-raiser is based on the Victor Hugo play in which the commoner Ruy Blas is forced to dishonour the Queen of Spain by winning her affections.

Broadcast
RADIO Live on Radio 3
ONLINE Live and 'listen again' options at bbc.co.uk/proms

Spotlight on ... Lars Vogt

Brahms's Second Piano Concerto may not sound as technically challenging as his First but, says pianist Lars Vogt, 'it's a hundred times more difficult. In the last movement there are ridiculous difficulties in almost every page.'

Vogt identifies two sides to the concerto: 'It begins with two dramatic movements with large orchestra, then there are two quite gentle movements, which feel more like chamber music. It's as if Brahms didn't want to return at the end to that earlier drama; a lot of the players could go home after the second movement.'

And he's pleased to be performing again with Jiří Bělohlávek. 'We did five memorable performances of the Brahms First Concerto together. He's a very open musician, but also a warm person, which makes a difference; ultimately we're all humans, aren't we?'

THURSDAY 24 JULY ♪

Proms Plus 5.45pm, Royal College of Music
Proms Intro Managing and Artistic Director of the English Music Festival, Em Marshall, and pianist Ashley Wass discuss Bax, Vaughan Williams and English music with Petroc Trelawny.
Free to ticket-holders. Edited version will be available at bbc.co.uk/proms

7.30pm–c9.25pm, Royal Albert Hall

Bax
In memoriam Patrick Pearse *15'*
first public performance

Rachmaninov
Piano Concerto No. 1
in F sharp minor *26'*

interval

Vaughan Williams
Symphony No. 4 in F minor *33'*

Yevgeny Sudbin *piano*

BBC Philharmonic
Yan Pascal Tortelier *conductor*

Yevgeny Sudbin

Yan Pascal Tortelier returns to the Manchester-based BBC Philharmonic, of which he is Conductor Laureate, for a programme that includes the first public performance of Arnold Bax's *In memoriam* – a short orchestral work written in memory of Patrick Pearse, a leader of the failed Irish Easter Rising in 1916. The piece was only recently discovered to have been orchestrated and shows Bax at his most inventive. Vaughan Williams's Fourth (which he dedicated to Bax) is one of his most powerful symphonies, showing a very different side to the composer from the serene, pastoral idiom with which he is often associated. And between these two British works, the first of Rachmaninov's four piano concertos. At its heart lies a slow movement of great beauty – a poetic gift for the astoundingly talented Yevgeny Sudbin, making his Proms debut. See 'Two-Way Vision', pages 12–17; 'A New Encounter', pages 34–35

Broadcast
RADIO Live on Radio 3
ONLINE Live and 'listen again' options at bbc.co.uk/proms

WEEKEND PROMMING PASS – BEAT THE QUEUES AND SAVE MONEY (SEE PAGE 136)

FRIDAY 25 JULY ♪

Proms Plus 5.45pm, Royal College of Music
Proms Composer Portrait Simon Holt, in conversation with Radio 3's Sarah Walker, discusses his new Proms commission and introduces performances of some of his chamber works.
Free to all. Edited broadcast on Radio 3 later this evening

7.30pm–c9.25pm, Royal Albert Hall

Debussy
Nocturnes   *25'*

Simon Holt
Troubled Light   *c21'*
BBC commission: world premiere

interval

Musorgsky, orch. Ravel
Pictures at an Exhibition   *30'*

Cantamus Girls' Choir
BBC National Orchestra of Wales
Thierry Fischer *conductor*

The first of this season's BBC commissions marks the 50th-birthday year of recent British Composer Award-winner Simon Holt. His *Troubled Light* explores descriptions of colour by poets and artists. There's more colour from Debussy – his delicate and exquisite *Nocturnes*, an aural response to James McNeill Whistler's canvases – diffuse, evocative and strikingly original. The youthful voices of Cantamus join the BBC National Orchestra of Wales for the closing 'Sirènes', a dream-like evocation of a magical seascape. And rich orchestral colour, courtesy of another Frenchman, comes with perhaps the most famous orchestration of them all, Maurice Ravel's of Musorgsky's *Pictures at an Exhibition*. The individual paintings from the Russian's stroll around an art gallery receive a vibrant new lease of life when stretched on to this huge orchestral canvas.
See 'New Music', pages 42–49

Broadcast
RADIO Live on Radio 3
ONLINE Live and 'listen again' options at bbc.co.uk/proms

SATURDAY 26 JULY ♪

Proms Plus 5.15pm, Royal College of Music
Proms Intro Young Composers Winners' Day Tom Service discusses *Tevot*, alongside live performances of commissions by the winners of the 2007 Proms Inspire Young Composers' Competition.
Free to all.

7.00pm–c9.40pm, Royal Albert Hall

Musorgsky
A Night on the Bare Mountain
('Sorochintsy Fair' version, 1880)   *12'*

Boris Godunov – Coronation Scene;
Boris's Monologue; Death Scene   *25'*

interval

Thomas Adès
Tevot   *23'*

interval

Prokofiev
Piano Concerto No. 1 in D flat major   *15'*

Borodin
Polovtsian Dances   *13'*

Sir John Tomlinson *bass*
Louis Lortie *piano*

City of Birmingham Symphony Youth Chorus
City of Birmingham Symphony Chorus
City of Birmingham Symphony Orchestra
Thomas Adès *conductor*

Sir John Tomlinson

Polymath Thomas Adès – composer, pianist, festival director and conductor – presides over this epic evening of orchestral splendour with a distinct Russian flavour. From the diabolic slumber party of Musorgsky's *A Night on the Bare Mountain*, via the rhythmic vitality of Prokofiev's First Piano Concerto to Borodin's ever popular *Polovtsian Dances*, orchestral virtuosity features large. At the heart of the programme is Adès's own British Composer Award-winning *Tevot* – a work written for Sir Simon Rattle and the Berliner Philharmoniker, which explores 'the idea of the ship of the world' (one of tevot's meanings is 'ark'). Celebrated bass Sir John Tomlinson reprises his magnificent Boris in scenes from Musorgsky's opera.

Spotlight on ... Thomas Adès

Though aged only 37, Thomas Adès first had his music performed at the Proms 13 years ago, with eight further works appearing since then. In more recent years, like Oliver Knussen and George Benjamin before him, he has established a reputation as a conductor/director of rare insight. For tonight's Prom he is surrounding his own *Tevot* with some personal favourites from the Russian repertoire.

'These pieces,' he says, 'are like golden, precious objects from childhood. The Prokofiev concerto, for example, gives me that indescribable feeling that only comes from things we grow to love before reaching a certain age. It's only later in life that we want to explain their impact. There's an overwhelming excitement in the piece and a sort of magical clarity. The other works are all about intense, passionate themes – life and death, good and evil, justice and injustice, exile and return. Again, all set in that bright, hard Russian light.'

Broadcast
RADIO Live on Radio 3
ONLINE Live and 'listen again' options at bbc.co.uk/proms

SUNDAY 27 JULY ✕

11.00am–c1.00pm, Royal Albert Hall

Doctor Who Prom

Programme to include:

Murray Gold
Music from the Doctor Who series*   c40'

Copland
Fanfare for the Common Man   3'

Holst
The Planets – Jupiter   8'

Mark-Anthony Turnage
The Torino Scale   4'
UK premiere

Wagner
Die Walküre – The Ride of the Valkyries   5'

Freema Agyeman *presenter*

London Philharmonic Choir
BBC Philharmonic
Ben Foster*, Stephen Bell *conductors*

A family concert featuring music from the BBC's *Doctor Who* series, and including a specially filmed scene, written by Russell T Davies and starring David Tennant. There's also a selection of classical favourites with a strong flavour of time and space. Join Freema Agyeman (aka Martha Jones), and others from the *Doctor Who* cast, for an intergalactic musical adventure – with a little help from Daleks, Cybermen and other aliens from the series!

There will be one interval

Spotlight on ... Freema Agyeman

"I am really looking forward to the Doctor Who Prom – there will be Daleks and Cybermen walking around: they're just as menacing in real life! My clearest childhood memory of *Doctor Who* is the theme tune. I was over the moon that they didn't change it for the new series – I think people realised that it was as much a part of the programme as the Tardis. I was in the audience at the *Doctor Who* concert at the Cardiff Millennium Centre in 2006, in aid of BBC Children in Need. There were lots of families around me who hadn't spotted me. It was only because there was a TV camera that was roaming the crowds, beaming images to a screen, that everyone realised I was there. At least at the Prom, everyone will know where I am!"

Broadcast
RADIO Live on Radio 3
ONLINE Live and 'listen again' options at bbc.co.uk/proms
TV Recorded for future broadcast on BBC One

Proms Plus 2.00pm, Royal College of Music
Proms Family Orchestra Join the Proms Family Orchestra for an afternoon session inspired by music from the Doctor Who Prom
Free to all. See page 67 for details

SUNDAY 27 JULY ✕

Proms Plus 5.15pm, Royal College of Music
Proms Intro A Romantic modernist – Messiaen's music from the vantage point of *La Transfiguration*, with Dr Christopher Dingle and musicians from the RCM, presented by Tom Service.
Free to ticket-holders.

7.00pm–c8.50pm, Royal Albert Hall

Messiaen
La Transfiguration de Notre
Seigneur Jésus-Christ   98'

Dénes Várjon *piano*
Adam Walker *flute*
Julian Bliss *clarinet*
Sonia Wieder-Atherton *cello*
Colin Currie *xylophone*
Adrian Spillett *marimba*
Richard Benjafield *vibraphone*

BBC Symphony Chorus
BBC National Chorus of Wales
BBC National Orchestra of Wales
Thierry Fischer *conductor*

Composed in the mid-1960s, *La Transfiguration de Notre Seigneur Jésus-Christ* marked Olivier Messiaen's return to writing for voices after a break of 17 years. The work is inspired by Christ's transfiguration as reported in the Gospels of Matthew, Mark and Luke: the moment when he is suffused with light, speaks with Moses and Elijah, and is named the Son of God. This huge score, with seven instrumental soloists, a choir of 200 and a vast orchestra, is one of Messiaen's most imposing and powerful creations, a fervent expression of his passionately held Roman Catholic faith – and highlight of this year's Proms Messiaen-centenary celebrations. See 'The Light of Sound', pages 20–25

There will be no interval

Broadcast
RADIO Live on Radio 3
ONLINE Live and 'listen again' options at bbc.co.uk/proms
TV Broadcast at 7.30pm on BBC Four

BBC

MONDAY 28 JULY

1.00pm–c2.00pm

Proms Chamber Music at Cadogan Hall

Monteverdi

Volgendo il ciel   *11'*

Arianna – Lamento d'Arianna   *12'*

Il ballo delle ingrate   *25'*

I Fagiolini
Barokksolistene
Robert Hollingworth *director*

All that has survived of Monteverdi's great second opera, *Arianna* – whose 400th anniversary falls in 2008 – is Arianna's Lament, which became so famous that, 40 years later, it was said to be on the shelves of every serious musician. Its arrangement for five voices stands as a pinnacle of Italian madrigal-writing. The opening and closing works this lunchtime are the dance-inspired pieces that end the two parts of Monteverdi's Eighth Book of Madrigals: the first, *Volgendo il ciel*, representing War, the second, *Il ballo delle ingrate*, reflecting Love.

There will be no interval

I Fagiolini

Broadcast
RADIO Live on Radio 3
ONLINE Live and 'listen again' options at bbc.co.uk/proms

MONDAY 28 JULY

Proms Plus 5.45pm, Royal College of Music
Proms Intro Writer and critic Paul Griffiths joins conductor David Robertson and oboist Nicholas Daniel, with presenter Andrew McGregor, to discuss the music of Elliott Carter.
Free to ticket-holders. Edited version will be available at bbc.co.uk/proms

7.30pm–c9.15pm, Royal Albert Hall

Beethoven

Grosse Fuge   *17'*

Elliott Carter

Oboe Concerto   *21'*

interval

Beethoven

Symphony No. 5 in C minor   *32'*

Nicholas Daniel *oboe*

BBC Symphony Orchestra
David Robertson *conductor*

As well as marking Elliott Carter's centenary, tonight's Prom celebrates the 200th anniversary of Beethoven's Fifth Symphony, premiered in 1808. Carter's single-movement Oboe Concerto from 1986–7 finds, in the composer's words, 'the soloist accompanied in its widely varying, mercurial moods  by a percussionist and four violas'. Apart from opening with the most famous motif in the whole of Western music, Beethoven's Fifth is a study in coiled tension and release that never fails to thrill. And to open the evening, the full-string version of Beethoven's muscular *Grosse Fuge*, originally written as the composer's first thoughts for one of his late, great string quartets. *See 'Modernism with Soul', pages 38–39*

Nicholas Daniel

Broadcast
RADIO Live on Radio 3
ONLINE Live and 'listen again' options at bbc.co.uk/proms
TV Live on BBC Four. Beethoven Symphony No. 5 also recorded for broadcast on BBC Two on 6 September

Spotlight on ... David Robertson

The BBC Symphony Orchestra's Principal Guest Conductor, David Robertson, has a rare gift for devising eclectic and illuminating programmes. Both of the Beethoven pieces in tonight's Prom shocked audiences when they were first performed, and the arresting nature of the *Grosse Fuge* – less familiar to us than the Fifth Symphony – will, Robertson believes, help remind us that 'we've lost the sense of how radical Beethoven's Fifth Symphony really is. At the time it seemed completely incomprehensible to the public because of the enormous sense of forward movement in the very opening. Then it suddenly stops! Then it starts again, like some teenager trying to learn to drive, letting out the clutch too quickly and ramming into the parking wall.'

Carter, too, has been one of the most uncompromising composers of his own time, though his Oboe Concerto is essentially lyrical in character. 'The lyricism is also one of things you hear in the Beethoven symphony, and both these pieces have a sense of their ideas being tightly argued.' So Robertson's plan is that the *Grosse Fuge* 'sets the stage for what we'll hear in Beethoven's Fifth; and in between we have this pristine jewel in the Carter, which both prepares you for the symphony, and allows you to hear it differently.'

TUESDAY 29 JULY

Proms Plus 5.45pm, Royal College of Music
Proms Literary Festival Ian McMillan is joined by Professor Christopher Ricks and other guests, to take a new look at the poetry, life and times of A. E. Housman.
Free to ticket-holders. Edited broadcast on Radio 3 during tonight's interval

7.30pm–c9.40pm, Royal Albert Hall

Butterworth
A Shropshire Lad (orchestral rhapsody)   *12'*

Vaughan Williams
Symphony No. 8 in D minor   *30'*

interval

Bruch
Violin Concerto No. 1 in G minor   *25'*

R. Strauss
Till Eulenspiegels lustige Streiche   *15'*

Janine Jansen *violin*

Hallé
Mark Elder *conductor*

A British half and a German half – performed by an orchestra founded by a German but with a distinguished reputation in British music. Now in its 150th-anniversary season the Hallé, under Mark Elder, performs Vaughan Williams's 'little' Eighth Symphony – which this orchestra premiered in 1956. The poignant rhapsody by VW's friend George Butterworth gains extra resonance in the light of the latter's death in the First World War; it is introduced in tonight's performance with a reading from the Housman poems that inspired it. Following her stirring performance of Prokofiev's Violin Concerto No. 2 at the Proms last year, Janine Jansen joins the Hallé for the popular First Violin Concerto by Bruch (with whom Vaughan Williams studied). And, to close, Richard Strauss's colourful portrait of the scallywag Till Eulenspiegel. See 'Two-Way Vision', pages 12–17

Broadcast
RADIO Live on Radio 3
ONLINE Live and 'listen again' options at bbc.co.uk/proms
TV Butterworth, Bruch and Vaughan Williams recorded for broadcast on BBC Two on 2 August

WEDNESDAY 30 JULY

Proms Plus 5.15pm, Royal College of Music
Proms Intro Lucy Duran introduces tonight's world music award-winners in conversation with Rita Ray; plus a tribute to Andy Palacio, Americas Award-winner 2008, who died earlier this year.
Free to ticket-holders. Edited broadcast on Radio 3 during tonight's interval

7.00pm–c10.45pm, Royal Albert Hall

World Music Celebration – the winners of the Radio 3 Awards for World Music

Mayra Andrade (Cape Verde)
Justin Adams (UK) &
   Juldeh Camara (Gambia)
Bassekou Kouyate (Mali)
Sa Ding Ding (China)
Son de la Frontera (Spain)

Now in its seventh year, the Radio 3 Awards for World Music has established itself as a major event in the international music calendar, and this year the Proms welcomes its winners for the first time. The 11 categories of the Awards embrace music reflecting a kaleidoscopic range of cultural traditions from around the world – so we have Cape Verdean songs from **Mayra Andrade** (Newcomer); desert blues from **Justin Adams** and **Juldeh Camara** (Culture Crossing); the sounds of the Malian *ngoni* (a kind of lute) from **Bassekou Kouyate** (Africa and Album of the Year); Chinese electronica from **Sa Ding Ding** (Asia/Pacific); and flamenco fusion from **Son de la Frontera** (Europe). A chance to hear these winners live in concert and discover some of the most enticing sounds from across the planet.

In collaboration with Serious

There will be two intervals

Broadcast
RADIO Live on Radio 3
ONLINE Live and 'listen again' options at bbc.co.uk/proms
TV Recorded for broadcast in two parts on BBC Four on 4 August and 18 August

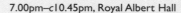

Mayra Andrade

Bassekou Kouyate

Sa Ding Ding

Spotlight on …
Radio 3 Awards for World Music

The Radio 3 Awards for World Music is a celebration of music and musicians from every corner of the globe, and Rita Ray, Chair of the jury, offers a flavour of what to expect at the award-winners' Prom. 'We love the way Son de la Frontera takes the flamenco tradition forward. It is very classic, yet sounds fresh and progressive. Bassekou Kouyate plays the *ngoni*, a West-African grandfather of the banjo; his quartet sounds even more scintillating live than on its last stunning album. Sa Ding Ding mixes traditional Chinese instruments with digital beats, keyboards and electric guitars; and the outrageously talented Mayra Andrade is from Cape Verde, but you can hear Brazil, Africa and Parisian jazz in her songs. The different roots of both Justin Adams and Juldeh Camara can be heard in their extraordinary music, yet they combine to create something really fresh.'

THURSDAY 31 JULY

Proms Plus 5.00pm, Royal College of Music
Proms Intro Emmanuelle Haïm discusses tonight's opera with Suzy Klein, followed by a presentation of the Orchestra of the Age of Enlightenment's and Glyndebourne's *Poppaea* film project.
Free to ticket-holders. Edited version will be available at bbc.co.uk/proms

7.00pm–c10.30pm, Royal Albert Hall

Monteverdi

The Coronation of Poppaea   *165'*
(semi-staged; sung in Italian)

Glyndebourne Festival Opera

Sonya Yoncheva *Fortune*
Simona Mihai *Virtue*
Amy Freston *Cupid*
Christophe Dumaux *Otho*
Alice Coote *Nero*
Danielle de Niese *Poppaea*
Wolfgang Ablinger-Sperrhacke *Arnalta*
Tamara Mumford *Octavia*
Marie Arnet *Drusilla*
Paolo Battaglia *Seneca*
Trevor Scheunemann *Mercury/Consul*
Patrick Schramm *Lictor/Consul*
Dominique Visse *Nurse/Friend*
Claire Ormshaw *Lady-in-Waiting*
Lucia Cirillo *Page*
Andrew Tortise *Lucan/Soldier 1/Tribune/Friend*
Peter Gijsbertsen *Liberto/Soldier 2/Tribune*

Orchestra of the Age of Enlightenment
Emmanuelle Haïm *conductor*

Alice Coote

Danielle de Niese

As well as being one of the first operas ever composed, Monteverdi's *Coronation of Poppaea* stands as one of the most psychologically acute and powerful dramatic works ever written. A specially devised semi-staging, based on Glyndebourne's new production, comes to the Proms under the dynamic direction of Emmanuelle Haïm. At the core of this battle of emotional wills is the magnificent trio of Christophe Dumaux, Alice Coote and – the soprano who won Prommers' hearts in 2005 as the temptress Cleopatra in Glyndebourne's *Julius Caesar* – Danielle de Niese.

There will be one interval

Spotlight on ... Emmanuelle Haïm

"The most striking characteristic of *The Coronation of Poppaea* is the modernity of the subject: even though it was written in the 17th century and is based on historical characters, you can identify with the characters very closely. This is Monteverdi's last opera and, unlike his more poetic opera *Orfeo*, it is gritty and violent, full of lust and scorned lovers. There is very little left of the opera in the surviving manuscripts: a bass line and the singers' parts. The instrumentation isn't there – we have to go on what was the practice of the time: organ, harpsichord, lute, harp, viola da gambas and a few violins and cellos. Working with a 'period' orchestra like the Orchestra of the Age of Enlightenment really helps, because they understand the music of this time. I have held one of the two remaining manuscripts and I was struck how small it was. So much music in such a small book!"

Broadcast
RADIO Live on Radio 3
ONLINE Live and 'listen again' options at bbc.co.uk/proms

FRIDAY 1 AUGUST

Proms Plus 6.15pm, Royal College of Music
Proms Intro Martin Handley in discussion with RLPO Executive Director Andrew Cornall, Composer-in-the-House Kenneth Hesketh and conductor Vasily Petrenko. With musicians from the RCM.
Free to ticket-holders.

8.00pm–c10.05pm, Royal Albert Hall

Kenneth Hesketh

Graven Image   *c15'*
BBC/Royal Liverpool Philharmonic Orchestra co-commission: world premiere

Beethoven

Piano Concerto No. 4 in G major   *35'*

interval

Rachmaninov

Symphonic Dances   *35'*

Paul Lewis *piano*

Royal Liverpool Philharmonic Orchestra
Vasily Petrenko *conductor*

Paul Lewis

A visit in Liverpool's year as European Capital of Culture from the city's Philharmonic and their charismatic young Principal Conductor, Vasily Petrenko. He brings a native's ear to Rachmaninov's bracing *Symphonic Dances*. He is joined by another young star for Beethoven's Fourth Piano Concerto – Paul Lewis, whose Beethoven credentials have been cemented by performing and recording the 32 piano sonatas to great acclaim. To start, a joint BBC/RLPO commission from the orchestra's Composer-in-the-House, the Liverpudlian Kenneth Hesketh, whose first work for the RLPO was premiered when he was only 19. See 'New Music', pages 42–49

Broadcast
RADIO Live on Radio 3
ONLINE Live and 'listen again' options at bbc.co.uk/proms

Stockhausen Day

One of the most influential composers of the 20th and 21st centuries, Karlheinz Stockhausen would have turned 80 this year. Aside from the performance of *Punkte* ('Points') by the Gürzenich Orchestra under Markus Stenz on the actual day that would have been the composer's 80th birthday (Prom 48), this Stockhausen Day offers a fuller immersion into the work of this uniquely uncompromising creative force. The early-evening Prom contrasts a pair of early works – *Gruppen* ('Groups', 1955–7), which passes ideas between three spatially separated ensembles, and *Kontakte* (1958–60), referring to 'contacts' between instrumental and electronic sounds – with two recent works – both of them excerpts from *Klang*, the large-scale sequence on which Stockhausen was working at the time of his death last December. In the Late Night Prom comes *Stimmung* for six amplified voices – the first work of Western music to be based on the harmonics, or overtones, that make up the sound-spectrum of a single note.

See 'Communing with the Cosmos', pages 28–31

Karlheinz Stockhausen

SATURDAY 2 AUGUST – STOCKHAUSEN DAY

Proms Plus Royal College of Music
1.00pm **Film** *Music Masters: Stockhausen* (48'); *In absentia* (23').
Double bill introduced by Robert Worby. **Free to all.**
4.15pm **Proms Intro** Ivan Hewett talks to Paul Hillier, Morag Grant, Robin Rimbaud and Robert Worby about Stockhausen.
Free to ticket-holders. Edited version will be available at bbc.co.uk/proms

6.00pm–c9.10pm, Royal Albert Hall

Stockhausen

Gruppen *24'*

Klang, 13th hour –
Cosmic Pulses (for electronics) *32'*
UK premiere

Klang, 5th hour –
Harmonien for solo trumpet *c15'*
BBC commission: world premiere

interval

Kontakte *35'*

Gruppen (repeat performance) *24'*

Marco Blaauw *trumpet*
Nicolas Hodges *piano*
Colin Currie *percussion*

BBC Symphony Orchestra
David Robertson *conductor*
Pascal Rophé *conductor*
Ludovic Morlot *conductor*

P P

Broadcast
RADIO Live on Radio 3
ONLINE Live and 'listen again' options at bbc.co.uk/proms

10.15pm–c11.35pm, Royal Albert Hall

Stockhausen

Stimmung *70'*

Theatre of Voices
Paul Hillier *director*

Theatre of Voices and Paul Hillier have already given us a magnificent recording of *Stimmung* (one which lends 'even more enchantment to this extraordinary work', in the words of *The Guardian*'s Andrew Clements). But this hypnotic piece for 'six singers and six microphones' takes on a unique atmosphere in live performance. Among the many influences which Stockhausen acknowledged when composing the work was a month spent wandering among the ruins in Mexico. The Theatre of Voices – as adept in music of the Middle Ages as in new music – have made something of a speciality of *Stimmung*, and Hillier's long association with the piece includes his participation as one of the singers at a Proms performance 30 years ago. One of several artists appearing more than once during this season, Hillier returns to conduct Rachmaninov's All-Night Vigil in Prom 36.

There will be no interval

SAME-DAY SAVER Book for both Proms 20 and 21 and save (see page 136)

Paul Hillier

Broadcast
RADIO Live on Radio 3
ONLINE Live and 'listen again' options at bbc.co.uk/proms

SUNDAY 3 AUGUST

4.00pm–c5.00pm, Royal Albert Hall

Demessieux
Te Deum 8'

Messiaen
Verset pour la Fête de la Dédicace 10'

Dupré
Symphony for Organ No. 2 17'

Naji Hakim
Pange lingua 9'

Messiaen
Prélude 9'

Organ improvisation c15'

Wayne Marshall organ

Wayne Marshall

Wayne Marshall returns after his festive First Night curtain-raiser (see Prom 1) with a programme celebrating the great French organ tradition. He also revives the seemingly lost art of the organ improvisation, so beloved of the great Gallic organ masters. Two works by Messiaen continue the centenary celebrations, while Dupré's magnificent Second Symphony for solo organ demonstrates the richness of his musical language – here's a symphony that really doesn't feel as if an orchestra is missing! The recital opens with the brief but moving Te Deum by Dupré's pupil Jeanne Demessieux, titulaire of the Madeleine in Paris for many years. And Messiaen's successor at La Trinité, Naji Hakim, is represented by his Pange lingua, a short work dating from 1996. See 'The Light of Sound', pages 20–25

There will be no interval

Broadcast
RADIO Live on Radio 3
ONLINE Live and 'listen again' options at bbc.co.uk/proms

SUNDAY 3 AUGUST

Proms Plus 5.45pm, Royal College of Music
Proms Literary Festival Susan Hitch discusses nature, wilderness and gardens with two poets for whom the pastoral is an important source of inspiration: Kathleen Jamie and Sarah Maguire.
Free to ticket-holders. Edited broadcast on Radio 3 during tonight's interval

7.30pm–c9.40pm, Royal Albert Hall

Beethoven
Symphony No. 1 in C major 27'

interval

Mahler
Das Lied von der Erde 65'

Karen Cargill mezzo-soprano
Johan Botha tenor

BBC Scottish Symphony Orchestra
Donald Runnicles conductor

Donald Runnicles, Scottish-born and newly appointed Chief Conductor of the BBC Scottish SO from September 2009, offers Mahler's symphony-with-voices, Das Lied von der Erde – a work that draws on Chinese poetry to magical effect. Worried by Das Lied's seemingly morose message, Mahler added some lines of his own about the

Karen Cargill

coming of spring and the renewal of life, and in doing so created one of the most intense closing passages in his entire output. 'Der Abschied' (The Farewell) is a challenge for any mezzo-soprano, but Karen Cargill (another Scot), as a former Kathleen Ferrier Award-winner, certainly has the pedigree. And in the tenor Johan Botha she has a partner of real vocal power. Beethoven's first essay in symphonic form makes a perfect opener to the evening.

SAME-DAY SAVER
Book for both Proms 22 and 23 and save (see page 136)

Broadcast
RADIO Live on Radio 3
ONLINE Live and 'listen again' options at bbc.co.uk/proms
TV Live on BBC Four

Spotlight on ... Donald Runnicles

Mahler's Das Lied von der Erde is famous for being the symphony Mahler was too superstitious to call his Ninth – Beethoven and Dvořák had both died before completing a Tenth. 'Mahler was deeply racked with uncertainty,' says Donald Runnicles. 'He had been diagnosed with heart disease and became obsessed by thoughts of death. There was a fashion at the time for Buddhism and Eastern philosophies in Vienna, and he was attracted to the serene answers they seemed to offer. This is probably why he was drawn to Chinese texts.'

Though the work is often viewed as a song-cycle, as Runnicles explains, 'it has the essence of a symphony. It doesn't have the traditional four movements, but the thematic structure uses a very symphonic, organic development. Achieving the correct balance between voice and orchestra is a challenge, and poses superhuman demands, particularly on the tenor.' Runnicles is happy to be working with Johan Botha, 'one of the finest tenors around', and is also pleased to be collaborating again with Karen Cargill, 'an extraordinary artist'.

MONDAY 4 AUGUST

1.00pm–c2.00pm

Proms Chamber Music at Cadogan Hall

Grieg
Violin Sonata No. 3   23'

Tchaikovsky
Sérénade mélancolique   8'

Souvenir d'un lieu cher   16'

Valse-Scherzo   5'

Julia Fischer *violin*
Yakov Kreizberg *piano*

Already an established partnership as soloist and conductor (which you can hear in Prom 25), Julia Fischer and Yakov Kreizberg here display their chamber-music rapport, with Fischer making her Proms debut. Their recent recording together of Tchaikovsky's Violin Concerto was a huge critical success and these three pieces for violin and piano come from the same period of his life – reflecting in their drama and melancholy a time of personal crisis intensified by the composer's disastrous marriage. Grieg's three violin sonatas were particularly dear to his heart and mirrored his development as a composer. He said the first was 'naive, rich in ideas', the second was 'national', and the third, which opens this concert, presented 'a wider horizon'.

There will be no interval

Broadcast
RADIO Live on Radio 3
ONLINE Live and 'listen again' options at bbc.co.uk/proms

MONDAY 4 AUGUST

Proms Plus 5.45pm, Royal College of Music
Proms Intro Margaret Reynolds talks to Roz Trübger and tonight's violinist Tasmin Little about the music of Dame Ethel Smyth, in the composer's 150th-anniversary year.
Free to ticket-holders. Edited version will be available at bbc.co.uk/proms

7.30pm–c9.55pm, Royal Albert Hall

Bach, orch. H. Wood
Toccata and Fugue in D minor, BWV 565   9'

Smyth
Concerto for Horn and Violin   28'

interval

Rachmaninov, orch. H. Wood
Prelude in C sharp minor   4'

Rachmaninov
Symphony No. 2 in E minor   62'

Richard Watkins *horn*
Tasmin Little *violin*

BBC Scottish Symphony Orchestra
Stefan Solyom *conductor*

Stefan Solyom

Born 150 years ago into an upper middle-class military London family, Ethel Smyth rebelled against her background to become not only one of the most successful British women composers but also an important figure in the suffragette movement. Her unusually scored concerto dates from 1927, when she was almost 70. It's a work she dedicated to Proms founder-conductor Henry Wood, whose large-scale arrangements we also hear tonight. An early champion of Rachmaninov in England, Wood conducted the Russian's richly Romantic Second Symphony at the Proms in 1924. See 'A New Encounter', pages 34–35

Broadcast
RADIO Live on Radio 3
ONLINE Live and 'listen again' options at bbc.co.uk/proms

TUESDAY 5 AUGUST

Proms Plus 5.15pm, Royal College of Music
Proms Literary Festival Matthew Sweet discusses how Victorian entertainment is portrayed in novels, films and television – with writer and critic John Sutherland and TV dramatist Andrew Davies.
Free to ticket-holders. Edited broadcast on Radio 3 on 7 August

7.00pm–c9.15pm, Royal Albert Hall

Wagenaar
Overture 'Cyrano de Bergerac'   14'

Dvořák
Symphony No. 6 in D major   45'

interval

Brahms
Violin Concerto in D major   42'

Julia Fischer *violin*

Netherlands Philharmonic Orchestra
Yakov Kreizberg *conductor*

Julia Fischer

Rustic dances provide energetic inspiration for the two large works this evening. Brahms's big-boned and technically demanding Violin Concerto ends with a wonderfully infectious peasant dance, while the third movement of Dvořák's Sixth employs the *furiant* with its thrilling cross-rhythms. Julia Fischer, *Gramophone* magazine's current Artist of the Year, is certainly among the ranks of today's most lavishly talented young violinists, and in Yakov Kreizberg she has a musical partner with whom she has made some outstanding recordings. To open the concert, the Netherlands Philharmonic brings the Straussian *Cyrano de Bergerac* overture by its compatriot Johan Wagenaar.

SAME-DAY SAVER
Book for both Proms 25 and 26 and save (see page 136)

Broadcast
RADIO Live on Radio 3
ONLINE Live and 'listen again' options at bbc.co.uk/proms

Karl-Magnus Fredriksson (Solyom); Kasskara (Fischer)

PROM 26

TUESDAY 5 AUGUST

10.15pm–c11.30pm, Royal Albert Hall

Poulenc
Chansons françaises, Op. 130 – selection   *11'*

John McCabe
Scenes in America deserta   *9'*

French Renaissance madrigals   *17'*
Lassus Dessus le marche d'Arras
Passereau Il est bel et bon
Lassus Toutes les nuits
Janequin La guerre

Victorian part-songs   *13'*
Rogers Hears not my Phyllis
Hobbs Phyllis is my only joy
Trad., arr. S. E. Lovatt The Little Green Lane
Bridge The Goslings

English folk songs   *13'*
Trad., arr. B. Chilcott Greensleeves
Trad., arr. G. Langford Blow away the morning dew
Trad., arr. P. Lawson The Turtle Dove
Trad., arr. G. Langford Widdicombe Fair

The King's Singers

The King's Singers return to the Proms, marking their 40th anniversary with a wide-ranging Anglo-French selection. Picking up on the flavour of our earlier Proms Folk Day (see Proms 4–5), the concert opens with six of Poulenc's set of eight French folk songs and ends with more recent arrangements – of the type The King's Singers have practically made their own – of traditional English songs. In between comes English music from the recent past and French music from further back in time.

There will be no interval

SAME-DAY SAVER
Book for both Proms 25 and 26 and save (see page 136)

PROM 27

WEDNESDAY 6 AUGUST

Proms Plus 5.30pm, Royal College of Music
Proms Intro Inspire Day The Aurora Orchestra performs the winning entries of this year's BBC Proms Inspire Young Composers' Competition.
Free to all. Edited broadcast on Radio 3 on 8 August

7.30pm–c9.45pm, Royal Albert Hall

Messiaen
L'Ascension (for orchestra)   *25'*

Stravinsky
Violin Concerto   *22'*

interval

George Benjamin
Ringed by the Flat Horizon   *20'*

Ravel
Pavane pour une infante défunte   *7'*

Boléro   *15'*

Carolin Widmann *violin*

BBC Symphony Orchestra
George Benjamin *conductor*

Carolin Widmann

A former pupil of Messiaen, Benjamin opens with *L'Ascension*, a sequence of meditations on religious themes. Carolin Widmann makes her Proms debut in Stravinsky's coolly neo-Classical concerto. Benjamin's own *Ringed by the Flat Horizon*, premiered while its composer was still a student at Cambridge, is dedicated to Messiaen and vividly depicts a storm brewing over a desolate New Mexico desert. The concert ends, as it began, in France, with one of Ravel's most limpid scores and one of his most popular. See 'The Light of Sound', pages 20–25

PROM 28

THURSDAY 7 AUGUST

Proms Plus 5.45pm, Royal College of Music
Family Music Intro Get a sneak preview of what's being played in tonight's Prom, and learn the stories behind the music. Bring your instrument for a chance to take part!
Free to ticket-holders

7.30pm–c9.45pm, Royal Albert Hall

Ferguson
Overture for an Occasion   *8'*

Stanford
Piano Concerto No. 2   *38'*

interval

Smetana
Má vlast – Vltava   *12'*

Dvořák
Symphony No. 8 in G major   *38'*

Finghin Collins *piano*

Ulster Orchestra
Kenneth Montgomery *conductor*

Finghin Collins

The Ulster Orchestra marks the centenary of Belfast-born Howard Ferguson with his lively *Overture for an Occasion*, a BBC commission from 1953. Young Irish pianist Finghin Collins makes his Proms debut in the richly Romantic Second Piano Concerto by the Dublin-born Charles Villiers Stanford, with whom Vaughan Williams studied. And to close, a second half from Central Europe, Smetana's popular portrait of the River Vltava and Dvořák's lively Eighth Symphony.

PROM 29

PROM 30

PROM 31

FRIDAY 8 AUGUST

Proms Plus 5.15pm, Royal College of Music
Proms Intro Composer Chen Yi and conductor Leonard Slatkin discuss tonight's programme, and wider Chinese cultural issues, with Sara Mohr-Pietsch.
Free to ticket-holders. Edited version will be available at bbc.co.uk/proms

7.00pm–c9.05pm, Royal Albert Hall

Chen Yi
Olympic Fire   c12'
BBC commission: world premiere

Rachmaninov
Rhapsody on a Theme of Paganini   24'

interval

Vaughan Williams
Five Variants of 'Dives and Lazarus'   12'

Symphony No. 6 in E minor   35'

Olga Kern *piano*

Royal Philharmonic Orchestra
Leonard Slatkin *conductor*

Commissioned to mark the opening of the Beijing Olympics today, Chen Yi's *Olympic Fire* looks forward to the London Olympics in 2012, evoking the image of fire and representing the idea of a meeting of cultures. Russian pianist Olga Kern, a Gold Medal-winner of the 2001 Van Cliburn International Piano Competition, plays the *Paganini Rhapsody* by Rachmaninov. To close, Leonard Slatkin – a longtime champion of Vaughan Williams – contrasts the sinuous *Five Variants of 'Dives and Lazarus'* with the Sixth Symphony. The latter was written between 1944 and 1949 and though VW denied it carried any particular narrative, many have seen it as his response to the atomic bombs that destroyed Hiroshima and Nagasaki. It's a work of violence, far removed from the pastoral voice with which he's so often associated. See 'Two-Way Vision', pages 12–17; 'A New Encounter', pages 34–35; New Music', pages 42–49

Broadcast
RADIO Live on Radio 3
ONLINE Live and 'listen again' options at bbc.co.uk/proms

FRIDAY 8 AUGUST

10.00pm–c11.20pm, Royal Albert Hall

Michael Torke
Javelin   8'

John Adams
The Chairman Dances   13'

Bernstein
Mass – Three Meditations   17'

Ellington
Harlem   16'

Han-Na Chang *cello*

BBC National Orchestra of Wales
Kristjan Järvi *conductor*

Tonight's Late Night Prom under the direction of the charismatic Kristjan Järvi celebrates 20th-century Americana. The Olympic theme takes to the sky with Michael Torke's most popular work, *Javelin*, a 1994 Olympics commission. John Adams's toe-tapping evocation of an earlier visit to Beijing and Duke Ellington's evocative *Harlem* offer two contrasting strands of 20th-century American music. And, in a more serene mood, cellist Han-Na Chang joins the orchestra for 'Three Meditations' from Leonard Bernstein's theatrical *Mass*.

There will be no interval

Kristjan Järvi

SAME-DAY SAVER Book for both Proms 29 and 30 and save (see page 136)

Broadcast
RADIO Live on Radio 3
ONLINE Live and 'listen again' options at bbc.co.uk/proms

SATURDAY 9 AUGUST

Proms Plus Royal College of Music
2.00pm Proms Family Orchestra The Proms Family Orchestra plays Jazz! See page 67 for details of how to sign up.
5.15pm Family Music Intro Learn more about tonight's jazz-based music. Music Intro event is free to ticket-holders

7.00pm–c9.00pm, Royal Albert Hall

Gershwin
Strike up the Band   7'

Gershwin, arr. Jason Yarde
Porgy and Bess – 'My man's gone now'   6'
BBC commission: world premiere

Jason Yarde
Rhythm and Other Fascinations   c6'
BBC commission: world premiere

Stravinsky
Ebony Concerto   10'

Bernstein
Prelude, Fugue and Riffs   10'

interval

Gwilym Simcock
Progressions for piano and orchestra   c22'
BBC commission: world premiere

Gershwin
An American in Paris   18'

Gwilym Simcock *piano*
Phil Donkin *double bass*
Martin France *drums*
Michael Collins *clarinet*

BBC Concert Orchestra
Charles Hazlewood *conductor*

Jazz infuses tonight's programme, with Gershwin's gift for melody opening and closing the evening. And there are new pieces by Radio 3 New Generation Artist Gwilym Simcock and Jason Yarde. See 'New Music', pages 42–49

Broadcast
RADIO Live on Radio 3
ONLINE Live and 'listen again' options at bbc.co.uk/proms
TV Live on BBC Two

Spotlight on ... Charles Hazlewood

"Gwilym Simcock has a wonderful knack of being able to do things right on the edge of possibility. So where some modern jazz is a bit scary, Gwilym's music has huge appeal to it, without ever losing integrity. It is great that the BBC Concert Orchestra is collaborating with him, as they can swing in a way that many other orchestras can't.

As for the other jazz-influenced composers in the Prom, Gershwin tried to sculpt an American musical vocabulary, somewhere between jazz and classical, a vocabulary that was definable as American and wasn't just inherited from across the pond in Europe. Bernstein went on to develop this language, but has suffered from having such success on Broadway – including *West Side Story*, *Candide* and *On the Town* – that his more 'serious' compositions for the concert hall are sometimes forgotten. As for Stravinsky, who spent the end of his life in America, it would have been very strange if he hadn't been excited by the language of jazz – and just listen to the vitality of his rhythms."

SUNDAY 10 AUGUST

4.00pm–c5.00pm, Royal Albert Hall

Messiaen
Messe de la Pentecôte   29'

interspersed with

Manchicourt
Missa 'Veni Creator Spiritus'   26'

James O'Donnell organ

BBC Singers
Andrew Carwood conductor

Ancient meets modern, as Messiaen's *Mass for Pentecost*, for solo organ – here performed by Organist and Master of the Choristers at Westminster Abbey, James O'Donnell – is interspersed with music from the 16th century. The Missa *Veni Creator Spiritus* by the Franco-Flemish Pierre de Manchicourt – a composer at last receiving the attention he deserves – offers a change of pace and texture. Andrew Carwood, a much-lauded specialist in the music of the Renaissance, leads the BBC Singers through this haunting music. See 'The Light of Sound', pages 20–25

There will be no interval

Andrew Carwood

Broadcast
RADIO Live on Radio 3
ONLINE Live and 'listen again' options at bbc.co.uk/proms

SUNDAY 10 AUGUST

Proms Plus 5.45pm, Royal College of Music
Proms Intro Tonight's conductor, Edward Gardner, talks to composers Michael Berkeley and Stuart MacRae, whose new works he will be conducting tonight. Ivan Hewett hosts.
Free to ticket-holders. Edited version will be available at bbc.co.uk/proms

7.30pm–c9.30pm, Royal Albert Hall

Sibelius
Night Ride and Sunrise   15'

Michael Berkeley
Slow Dawn   c6'
world premiere of new version

Stuart MacRae
Gaudete   c28'
BBC commission: world premiere

interval

Elgar
Enigma Variations   30'

Susanna Andersson soprano

BBC Symphony Orchestra
Edward Gardner conductor

SAME-DAY SAVER
Book for both Proms 32 and 33 and save (see page 136)

The young Music Director of English National Opera, Edward Gardner, gives the premieres of two British works: Stuart MacRae's nature-inspired *Gaudete* and Michael Berkeley's revisiting of his *Slow Dawn*, which he describes as depicting 'the gradual appearance of the sun (in the form of the tuba) as it climbs into the sky. Shafts of light and playful reflections accompany the increasing warmth of day.' The sun theme first arises in Sibelius's evocative *Night Ride and Sunrise*, a typically brooding tone-poem. Elgar's affectionate sketches of his 'friends pictured within' have caught the imaginations of thousands over the past 100 years. See 'New Music', pages 42–49

Broadcast
RADIO Live on Radio 3
ONLINE Live and 'listen again' options at bbc.co.uk/proms

MONDAY 11 AUGUST

1.00pm–c2.00pm

Proms Chamber Music at Cadogan Hall

Messiaen

Harawi 56'

Gweneth-Ann Jeffers *soprano*
Simon Lepper *piano*

Gweneth-Ann Jeffers

Olivier Messiaen wrote this extended song-cycle as the first in a trilogy of works inspired by the legend of Tristan and Isolde (the others – *Cinq rechants* and the *Turangalîla Symphony* – can be heard in Proms 63 and 64 respectively). Unlike the majority of Messiaen's music, these works explore human, rather than divine, love: there is no mention of God anywhere in them. *Harawi* alludes to Peruvian love songs, even though the texts to the 12 songs are by Messiaen himself. Gweneth-Ann Jeffers, a former member of the Young Artists Programme at the Royal Opera House, is developing a formidable reputation, and Simon Lepper has become a sought-after partner for a number of rising-star singers. *See 'The Light of Sound', pages 20–25*

There will be no interval

See 'The Light of Sound', pages 20–25

Broadcast
RADIO Live on Radio 3
ONLINE Live and 'listen again' options at bbc.co.uk/proms

MONDAY 11 AUGUST

Proms Plus 5.45pm, Royal College of Music
Proms Intro Suzy Klein discusses tonight's opera, Puccini's *Il tabarro*, with musicologists Roger Parker and Alexandra Wilson.
Free to ticket-holders. Edited broadcast on Radio 3 during tonight's interval

7.30pm–c9.50pm, Royal Albert Hall

Rachmaninov

Symphony No. 1 in D minor 47'

interval

Puccini

Il tabarro *(concert performance; sung in Italian)* 55'

Barbara Frittoli *Giorgetta*
Miro Dvorsky *Luigi*
Lado Ataneli *Michele*
Jane Henschel *La Frugola*
Barry Banks *Il 'Tinca'*
Alastair Miles *Il 'Talpa'*
Allan Clayton *Ballad-seller*
Katherine Broderick *Young Lover*
Edgaras Montvidas *Young Lover*

BBC Singers
BBC Philharmonic
Gianandrea Noseda *conductor*

Gianandrea Noseda

A concert that combines two of Gianandrea Noseda's enthusiasms – an opera from his native Italy and a symphony from the country where he studied conducting (under Valery Gergiev). Rachmaninov's rarely heard First Symphony is followed by the first panel of the operatic triptych *Il trittico* by Puccini (born 150 years ago). Soprano Barbara Frittoli takes the role of Giorgetta, the barge-owner's wife whose straying fidelity leads to fatal consequences for her lover Luigi. *See 'A New Encounter', pages 34–35*

See 'A New Encounter', pages 34–35

Broadcast
RADIO Live on Radio 3
ONLINE Live and 'listen again' options at bbc.co.uk/prom

Spotlight on ... Barbara Frittoli

Barbara Frittoli made her Proms debut in 2003 singing Strauss's *Four Last Songs* with tonight's orchestra and conductor, and this year she returns with the same musical partners, to sing Giorgetta in Puccini's tense *Il tabarro* ('The Cloak'). The unfulfilled younger wife of the barge-owner Michele, Giorgetta arouses deep-rooted suspicion and jealousy in her husband. 'I like Giorgetta,' declares Frittoli. 'She is a normal woman, but she is unfaithful to her husband owing to the deep sorrow of losing their child. In the end she decides to return to him, but by then it is too late.' Indeed, Michele uncovers her affair with Luigi and murders his rival. He wraps the body in the same cloak beneath which, in happier times, he would huddle together with Giorgetta and their now-dead child, to take shelter on cold nights. Puccini's score keenly reflects both the tale's dramatic realism and the murky undercurrents of the disturbed human psyche.

TUESDAY 12 AUGUST ⌐

Proms Plus 5.00pm, Royal College of Music
Proms Literary Festival Ben Haggarty explores the extraordinary world of the *1,001 Nights* in this family-friendly storytelling session.
Free to ticket-holders

7.00pm–c9.15pm, Royal Albert Hall

Elgar
In the South (Alassio) *22'*

Vaughan Williams
Piano Concerto in C major *26'*

interval

Rimsky-Korsakov
Sheherazade *45'*

Ashley Wass *piano*

BBC Philharmonic
Vassily Sinaisky *conductor*

A winter holiday on the Ligurian coast in northern Italy provided the inspiration for one of Elgar's most popular concert overtures, a work with surprisingly dark undertones. Vaughan Williams's rarely heard Piano Concerto has a fierce, rhythmically vital quality that relates it to the Fourth Symphony (Prom 10). The soloist is Ashley Wass, one of the younger-generation champions of the British piano repertoire. To end, marking the 100th anniversary of Rimsky-Korsakov's death, an evocation of tales from the *Arabian Nights* as told by the seductive princess Sheherazade. Vassily Sinaisky and the BBC Philharmonic have long been steeped in this richly coloured repertoire. See *'Two-Way Vision', pages 12–17*

TUESDAY 12 AUGUST ⌐

Proms Plus 9.15pm, Royal College of Music
Proms Literary Festival The Archbishop of Canterbury, Rowan Williams, joins Susan Hitch to talk about and introduce the work of one of his literary heroes: Fyodor Dostoyevsky.
Free to all: ticket required, available on the day at the RAH Box Office until 9.00pm and then on the door at the RCM. Edited broadcast on Radio 3 on 20 August

---

10.15pm–c11.30pm, Royal Albert Hall

Rachmaninov
All-Night Vigil (Vespers) *63'*

Estonian Philharmonic Chamber Choir
Paul Hillier *conductor*

Paul Hillier returns with his other choir (he directs Theatre of Voices in Stockhausen's *Stimmung* in Prom 21) for Rachmaninov's heartfelt setting of the Orthodox All-Night Vigil. Dating from shortly before the composer's departure from his native Russia, it is one of his finest achievements. Among the most accomplished choirs performing today, the Estonian Philharmonic Chamber Choir has garnered impressive reviews. Writing of its recording of this work, classicstoday.com said, 'these are exciting and often moving performances as the choir works the phrasing and dynamics into thoughtful, sincere expressions of the texts, never losing the effect and inherent Romanticism of Rachmaninov's gorgeous lines and rich harmonies.' See *'A New Encounter', pages 34–35*

There will be no interval

SAME-DAY SAVER
Book for both Proms 35 and 36 and save (see page 136)

WEDNESDAY 13 AUGUST

Proms Plus 5.45pm, Royal College of Music
Proms Composer Portrait Anders Hillborg, in conversation with Fiona Talkington, discusses his new Proms commission and introduces performances of some of his chamber works.
Free to all. Edited broadcast on Radio 3 later this evening

7.30pm–c9.50pm, Royal Albert Hall

Ravel
La valse *13'*

Anders Hillborg
Clarinet Concerto
(Peacock Tales) *28'*
UK premiere

Gustavo Dudamel

interval

Berlioz
Symphonie fantastique *55'*

Martin Fröst *clarinet*

Gothenburg Symphony Orchestra
Gustavo Dudamel *conductor*

Since his first appearance at the Proms – with the Gothenburg Symphony Orchestra – three years ago, Gustavo Dudamel has become one of the fastest-rising conductors around – and his sensational appearance last year with the Simón Bolívar Youth Orchestra of Venezuela was one of the season's highlights. Not only is he now Principal Conductor of tonight's Swedish orchestra, but next year he succeeds Esa-Pekka Salonen as Music Director of the Los Angeles Philharmonic. Here's a programme to demonstrate his charismatic baton technique – Ravel's heady evocation of a society in decay and Berlioz's arch-Romantic portrayal of obsessive love enclose the UK premiere of Swedish composer Anders Hillborg's Clarinet Concerto, played (as well as danced and mimed) by the sensational Martin Fröst. See *'New Music', pages 42–49*

THURSDAY 14 AUGUST

Proms Plus 5.15pm, Royal College of Music
Proms Intro Members of the West-Eastern Divan Orchestra talk to the Controller of BBC Radio 3 and Director of the Proms, Roger Wright.
Free to ticket-holders. Edited version will be available at bbc.co.uk/proms

---

7.00pm–c9.05pm, Royal Albert Hall

Haydn
Sinfonia concertante in B flat major, for oboe, bassoon, violin and cello *21'*

Schoenberg
Variations for Orchestra, Op. 31 *21'*

interval

Brahms
Symphony No. 4 in E minor *42'*

West-Eastern Divan Orchestra
Daniel Barenboim *conductor*

THURSDAY 14 AUGUST

10.15pm–c11.30pm, Royal Albert Hall

Pierre Boulez
Mémoriale ('… explosante-fixe …' Originel) *6'*

Stravinsky
L'histoire du soldat *60'*

Members of the
West-Eastern Divan Orchestra
Daniel Barenboim *conductor*

Written during the First World War, 'to be read, played and danced', *L'histoire du soldat* ('The Soldier's Tale') presents the Faustian tale of a soldier who is tricked by the Devil into trading his fiddle for a book containing the secret of wealth. Boulez's … *explosante-fixe* … – from which *Mémoriale* is derived – was written to commemorate the death of Stravinsky in 1971. The *Mémoriale* realisation (1985) was prompted by the death of Lawrence Beauregard, flautist of Boulez's Ensemble Intercontemporain.

There will be no interval

SAME-DAY SAVER
Book for both Proms 38 and 39 and save (see page 136)

Spotlight on … Daniel Barenboim

Barenboim's West-Eastern Divan Orchestra, formed in collaboration with the Palestinian philosopher Edward Said, began life in 1999 as a one-off experiment to bring Arab and Israeli musicians together. Since then it has met in the summers to continue its work – both musical and social. While the symbolic effect of joining people on both sides of the Arab-Israeli conflict remains potent, the orchestra has been in continual artistic development. 'The "exotic" element, if you like,' says Barenboim, 'of an orchestra of Israelis and Arabs performing European music has lessened. This is a positive thing: the orchestra is now judged purely on musical terms.' Barenboim is proud too that, with the help of scholarships, around 30 of his young players have been able to study in Europe during the winter, before returning to the West-Eastern Divan for summer rehearsals. 'Three of our members are now in the Berliner Philharmoniker, and the oboist who will play in the Haydn *Sinfonia concertante* at the Proms is the Principal Oboe of the Bavarian Radio Symphony Orchestra.'

West-Eastern Divan Orchestra

Broadcast
RADIO Live on Radio 3
ONLINE Live and 'listen again' options at bbc.co.uk/proms
TV Broadcast at 7.30pm on BBC Four. Highlights also recorded for broadcast on BBC Two on 16 August

Broadcast
RADIO Live on Radio 3
ONLINE Live and 'listen again' options at bbc.co.uk/proms

Bleu Doalin (Barenboim): Chris Christodoulou/Lebrecht Music & Arts (West-Eastern Divan)

FRIDAY 15 AUGUST

Proms Plus Royal College of Music
1.00pm Film *The Cunning Little Vixen* (75').
Animation by Geoff Dunbar, introduced by Geoffrey Chew.
5.45pm Proms Intro Tonight's conductor, Pierre Boulez,
discusses Janáček with Proms Director Roger Wright.
*Film: free to all. Proms Intro: free to ticket-holders; edited broadcast
on Radio 3 during tonight's interval*

7.30pm–c9.30pm, Royal Albert Hall

Janáček

Sinfonietta *23'*

Concertino *17'*

interval

Glagolitic Mass (original version,
reconstr. Paul Wingfield) *41'*

Jean-Efflam Bavouzet *piano*
Jeanne-Michèle Charbonnet *soprano*
Anna Stéphany *mezzo-soprano*
Simon O'Neill *tenor*
Peter Fried *bass*
Simon Preston *organ*

BBC Symphony Chorus
London Symphony Chorus
BBC Symphony Orchestra
Pierre Boulez *conductor*

The music of Leoš Janáček is a relatively recent
departure for Pierre Boulez, who conducted *From
the House of the Dead* at the Aix-en-Provence Festival
last year to great acclaim. Here he takes on two of the
Czech composer's greatest non-theatrical works, as
well as the rarely encountered *Concertino* for piano
and orchestra. The *Sinfonietta*, with its extraordinary
brassy sonorities, shares the first half with the *Concertino*.
The *Glagolitic Mass* – featuring Simon Preston, who
later returns for his Bach Day recital (Prom 50) – is
visceral in its orchestration, and is here restored to
Janáček's more fiery and dramatic original version.

Broadcast
RADIO Live on Radio 3
ONLINE Live and 'listen again' options at bbc.co.uk/proms
TV Live on BBC Four. Highlights also recorded for broadcast on
BBC Two on 16 August

SATURDAY 16 AUGUST

Proms Plus 4.45pm, Royal College of Music
Proms Intro Catherine Bott talks to critic, writer and
broadcaster Roderick Swanston and theatre historian
Sarah Lenton to explore Handel's *Belshazzar*.
Free to ticket-holders. Edited broadcast on Radio 3 during tonight's interval

6.30pm–c10.00pm, Royal Albert Hall

Handel

Belshazzar *172'*

Paul Groves *Belshazzar*
Rosemary Joshua *Nitocris*
Bejun Mehta *Cyrus*
Iestyn Davies *Daniel*
Robert Gleadow *Gobrias*

Choir of the Enlightenment
Orchestra of the Age of Enlightenment
Sir Charles Mackerras *conductor*

Sir Charles Mackerras returns to the Proms with one
of his greatest loves, the music of George Frideric
Handel. Dating from 1744, when Handel's creativity as
a composer was at its peak, *Belshazzar* was written
simultaneously with another oratorio, *Hercules* – and
at colossal speed (he finished the work in a month).
It's based on the famous Old Testament story telling
of the downfall of the Babylonian king. But Handel's
libretto, by Charles Jennens, was considerably expanded
with numerous incidents imported from other sources.

The work was first heard at the King's Theatre in
London in March 1745 (though the indisposition of
one of its star performers meant that various of the
solos had to be redistributed among other members
of the cast, apparently rather unsatisfactorily).

Belshazzar is a work of consummate dramatic unity,
wonderfully structured and perfectly paced, in
which Handel skilfully characterises the three peoples
portrayed – the Babylonians, the Jews and the Persians.

There will be one interval

Broadcast
RADIO Live on Radio 3
ONLINE Live and 'listen again' options at bbc.co.uk/proms

Spotlight on ... Sir Charles Mackerras

Sir Charles Mackerras is one of the relatively
few conductors who have managed successfully
to straddle both the Romantic orchestral
repertoire and music of the Baroque and
Classical periods. Conducting the Orchestra of
the Age of Enlightenment gives him particular
enjoyment, because, as he explains, 'they have
specially studied the style in which earlier music
was played. The string players bow and wind
players play in a completely different way
from that of a modern orchestra, so they
sound totally different.'

'It's one of the most dramatic of Handel's
oratorios,' says Sir Charles of *Belshazzar*. 'It's
difficult to choose a favourite moment – there
are so many – but there is the most marvellous
description in music of the writing on the wall,
which Daniel eventually translates.'

Though he tries to recreate the original
sounds of Baroque and Classical period-style
playing, he admits 'it's not an authentic concept
to have a conductor waving a baton for a
Handel oratorio: even quite large orchestras in
those days wouldn't have had what we think of
as a conductor; usually the director played the
harpsichord or the organ. I often wonder how
on earth they kept the music together!'

PROM 42	PRICE BAND **D**	PROM 43	PRICE BAND **A**	PCM 5

WEEKEND PROMMING PASS – BEAT THE QUEUES AND SAVE MONEY (SEE PAGE 136)

SUNDAY 17 AUGUST ✕

Proms Plus 1.00pm, Royal College of Music
Film *Messiaen: La liturgie de cristal* (88'). A film by Olivier Mille introducing Messiaen's musical universe through a series of archive clips filmed between 1964 and 1987.
Free to all

4.00pm–c5.15pm, Royal Albert Hall

Messiaen
Apparition de l'église éternelle   *10'*
La Nativité du Seigneur   *57'*

Jennifer Bate *organ*

Organist Jennifer Bate has been one of Messiaen's staunchest British champions, and this year sees her performing his music all over the world. In the 1980s she recorded his complete organ works to considerable acclaim ('Bate's scholarly approach and fastidious playing are reason enough … to collect the complete set,' wrote the *BBC Music Magazine*) and her world-premiere recording of his last organ work, *Livre du Saint Sacrement*, won a Grand Prix du Disque. This afternoon she juxtaposes the *Apparition de l'église éternelle* with *La Nativité du Seigneur* – both works written in the 1930s. See 'The Light of Sound', pages 20–25

There will be no interval

Jennifer Bate with Messiaen

SAME-DAY SAVER Book for both Proms 42 and 43 and save (see page 136)

Broadcast
RADIO Live on Radio 3
ONLINE Live and 'listen again' options at bbc.co.uk/proms

SUNDAY 17 AUGUST ✕

Proms Plus 5.45pm, Royal College of Music
Proms Literary Festival Matthew Sweet goes on an urban safari – exploring the inspiration of wildness and nature in the city – with Iain Sinclair and Robert Macfarlane, author of *The Wild Places*.
Free to ticket-holders. Edited broadcast on Radio 3 on 18 August

---

7.30pm–c9.55pm, Royal Albert Hall

Mozart
Symphony No. 34 in C major, K338   *22'*

Vaughan Williams
Flos campi   *19'*

Nigel Osborne
Flute Concerto   *16'*

interval

Beethoven
Mass in C   *45'*

Rebecca Evans *soprano*
Pamela Helen Stephen *mezzo-soprano*
Thomas Walker *tenor*
Matthew Rose *bass*
Sharon Bezaly *flute*
Lawrence Power *viola*

BBC Singers
City of London Sinfonia
Richard Hickox *conductor*

A programme that plays to Richard Hickox's varied strengths and passions. He continues his advocacy of English music in two works written 55 years apart. Vaughan Williams's *Flos campi*, for solo viola and orchestra, displays VW's characteristically rich, sensuous orchestration. The Flute Concerto by Nigel Osborne (60 this year) is a work of vibrant imagination, and was premiered by Hickox with tonight's ensemble. Two Classical-period works complete the evening: Mozart's Symphony No. 34 and Beethoven's Mass in C, written for the Esterházy Court. See 'Two-Way Vision', pages 12–17

Broadcast
RADIO Live on Radio 3
ONLINE Live and 'listen again' options at bbc.co.uk/proms
TV Live on BBC Four

MONDAY 18 AUGUST ✕

1.00pm–c2.00pm

Proms Chamber Music at Cadogan Hall

Ortiz
Passamezzo antico; Folia; Ruggiero Romanesca; Passamezzo moderno   *10'*

Hume
A Souldiers March; Harke, harke; A Souldiers Resolution   *9'*

Marais
Pièces de viole, 3è livre – Prélude; Muzettes I/II; La sautillante   *11'*

Sanz
Jácaras; Canarios   *8'*

Marais
Couplets des Folies d'espagne   *14'*

Jordi Savall *bass viol/viola da gamba*
Rolf Lislevand *theorbo/guitar*

Jordi Savall makes his Proms debut with a programme that mixes the intimate and the flamboyant. 'We revitalise ourselves in the past,' says Savall, and in this concert with his longtime collaborator Rolf Lislevand he celebrates the Renaisance and Baroque musical worlds of the Iberian peninsula – with a nod to the eccentricities of the English soldier and viol-player Tobias Hume. The sequence of folias and romanescas has its roots in lively folk dances, and the fantastic style of the music invites a high element of improvisation. Crowning it all is a virtuoso display-piece by Savall's great predecessor, the French Baroque gamba player, Marin Marais.

There will be no interval

Broadcast
RADIO Live on Radio 3
ONLINE Live and 'listen again' options at bbc.co.uk/proms

MONDAY 18 AUGUST

Proms Plus 5.45pm, Royal College of Music
Proms Intro Cellist Alban Gerhardt and musicologist David Nice in conversation with Martin Handley.

Free to ticket-holders. Edited version will be available at bbc.co.uk/proms

7.30pm–c9.35pm, Royal Albert Hall

Elliott Carter
Soundings   10'
UK premiere

Prokofiev
Symphony-Concerto   38'

interval

Beethoven
Symphony No. 6 in F major, 'Pastoral'   40'

Nicolas Hodges *piano*
Alban Gerhardt *cello*

BBC Scottish Symphony Orchestra
Ilan Volkov *conductor*

Alban Gerhardt

The second of the season's Elliott Carter premieres, marking the composer's centenary, brings a surprisingly humorous collaboration between conductor and pianist. Cellist Alban Gerhardt, one of the earliest members of Radio 3's New Generation Artists scheme, performs the challenging Symphony-Concerto that Prokofiev wrote for the legendary Rostropovich. The Russian cellist emphasised the work's lyricism – 'I do not know a composer with such beauty in his music' – a quality it shares with Beethoven's idyllic and dramatic 'Pastoral' Symphony. See *'Modernism with Soul'*, pages 38–39; *'New Music'*, pages 42–49

Broadcast
RADIO Live on Radio 3
ONLINE Live and 'listen again' options at bbc.co.uk/proms

TUESDAY 19 AUGUST

Proms Plus 5.15pm, Royal College of Music
Proms Intro The electronic music revolution – Jonathan Harvey talks to Andrew McGregor about how technology has introduced a radically new creative environment for today's composers.
Free to ticket-holders

7.00pm–c10.00pm, Royal Albert Hall

Jonathan Harvey
Tombeau de Messiaen   9'

Messiaen
Concert à quatre   26'

interval

Jonathan Harvey
Mortuos plango, vivos voco   9'

Speakings   c30'
BBC co-commission with IRCAM and Radio France: UK premiere

interval

Varèse
Poème électronique   8'

Déserts   24'

Cédric Tiberghien *piano*
Emily Beynon *flute*
Alexei Ogrintchouk *oboe*
Danjulo Ishizaka *cello*

BBC Scottish Symphony Orchestra
Ilan Volkov *conductor*

A rare opportunity to enter the electroacoustic sound-world. While Jonathan Harvey's UK premiere plays on the musical content of speech, his *Tombeau de Messiaen* is his homage to 'a great musical and spiritual presence' – represented tonight by the *Concert à quatre*, a work completed after Messiaen's death by his widow Yvonne Loriod. As well as Harvey's classic *Mortuos plango, vivos voco*, the concert features two works by one of the earliest pioneers of electronic music. See *'The Light of Sound'*, pages 20–25; *'New Music'*, pages 42–49

In collaboration with IRCAM

Ilan Volkov

Spotlight on ... Jonathan Harvey

Jonathan Harvey's *Speakings* is the latest in a line of works composed using the facilities of IRCAM, the cutting-edge computer-music research institute in Paris. The first of these pieces was the genre-defining *Mortuos plango, vivos voco* of 1980, which we also hear in tonight's Prom and which mixes the sound of the largest bell at Winchester Cathedral with that of the voice of Harvey's son, a chorister during the 1970s: Harvey often experienced the collision of these sounds while hearing the choir in rehearsal. The raw, recorded sounds, he says, 'were manipulated by computer and cross-bred with synthetic simulations of the same sounds. These latter could be internally transformed to an amazing degree: one could, for instance, move seamlessly from a vowel sung by the boy to the complex bell spectrum.'

Harvey is pleased to be sharing a programme with another musical innovator, Edgard Varèse. 'He was someone who single-mindedly, and bravely, didn't care for popular acclaim. He felt he had to create new things. These things take courage.'

Broadcast
RADIO Live on Radio 3
ONLINE Live and 'listen again' options at bbc.co.uk/proms

WEDNESDAY 20 AUGUST

Proms Plus 5.15pm, Royal College of Music
Proms Intro Christopher Cook talks to Director of the
Royal Ballet, Monica Mason, about the company, its history,
conductors and dancers.
Free to ticket-holders

7.00pm–c10.30pm, Royal Albert Hall

Tchaikovsky
The Sleeping Beauty *177'*

London Symphony Orchestra
Valery Gergiev *conductor*

Valery Gergiev

Valery Gergiev comes to the Proms with music from
his native Russia – music with more than a whiff of
the greasepaint that brings out the best in this
charismatic maestro. *The Sleeping Beauty* is one of
Tchaikovsky's most delicate and melodically rich ballet
scores – a perennial favourite that tells the story
of a handsome prince awakening a beautiful princess,
Aurora, thereby breaking the spell of the wicked
fairy Carabosse.

There will be one interval

Broadcast
RADIO Live on Radio 3
ONLINE Live and 'listen again' options at bbc.co.uk/proms

THURSDAY 21 AUGUST

Proms Plus 5.45pm, Royal College of Music
Proms Literary Festival How do writers portray classical music
in their work? Ian McMillan is joined by Conrad Williams, whose
novel *The Concert Pianist* is the story of a virtuoso musician in crisis.
Free to ticket-holders. Edited broadcast on Radio 3 on 23 August

7.30pm–c10.00pm, Royal Albert Hall

Dvořák
Slavonic Dances, Op. 46   *37'*

interval

Janáček
Osud *(concert performance; sung in Czech)*   *78'*

Cast includes:
Štefan Margita *Živný*
Amanda Roocroft *Míla*
Rosalind Plowright *Míla's Mother*
Aleš Briscein *Dr Suda*
Ailish Tynan *Miss Stuhlá*
Martina Bauerová *Miss Pacovská/Fanča*
George Longworth *Doubek (as a child)*

BBC Singers
BBC Symphony Orchestra
Jiří Bělohlávek *conductor*

Jiří Bělohlávek conducts music from his homeland:
Dvořák's infectiously vital *Slavonic Dances* – which
brought him to the attention of Brahms – and
Janáček's rarely heard *Osud* ('Fate'). This swift-moving
opera about the writing of an opera – with a luridly
melodramatic plot involving unmarried motherhood,
suicide, murder and madness – was not performed for
three decades after its composer's death but contains
some of Janáček's most inspired music. Štefan Margita
stars in the semi-autobiographical role of the
composer Živný, with Amanda Roocroft as both the
object of his obsessive love and the subject of his
long-gestated masterpiece.

Spotlight on ... Jiří Bělohlávek

"These two pieces are as different from one
another as one could imagine. Dvořák's most
joyful opus – his *Slavonic Dances* – is an incredibly
demanding task for any orchestra: it sounds like
light and uncomplicated music – and it really
should sound like that! – but to achieve this
lightness requires hard preparation.

Janáček's *Osud* does not have the popularity of
some of his better-known operas, but I am
convinced this is only because the story of the
opera is more complicated; from a musical point
of view, *Osud* is a highly imaginative and inspiring
work. It is about the unhappy fate of a young
couple, a composer called Živný and his beloved
Míla, who has a difficult life as the unmarried
mother of his child. Fate does not let their love
flourish, first because of society and family
restrictions, and later because of a fatal injury.
One can only speculate how much of Janáček's
own feelings are hidden behind these notes …"

Broadcast
RADIO Live on Radio 3
ONLINE Live and 'listen again' options at bbc.co.uk/proms

Advance Booking from 21 April • General Booking from 27 May: 0845 401 5040 *Calls from a BT landline are charged at local rate. Charges from mobiles and other networks may be higher*

WEEKEND PROMMING PASS – BEAT THE QUEUES AND SAVE MONEY (SEE PAGE 136)

FRIDAY 22 AUGUST

Proms Plus 5.15pm, Royal College of Music
Proms Intro Andrew McGregor introduces tonight's musical recreation, with oboist Tom Owen and Marketing Manager Lilly Schwerdtfeger and composer Colin Matthews.
Free to ticket-holders. Edited version will be available at bbc.co.uk/proms

7.00pm–c10.20pm, Royal Albert Hall

Mahler
Symphony No. 5 in C sharp minor   74'

interval

Stockhausen
Punkte (1952/1962/1993)   27'

interval

Schubert
Ständchen, D920b (orch. David Matthews)   6'

Bei dir allein, D866/2 (orch. Manfred Trojahn)   2'

Nacht und Träume, D827
(orch. Colin Matthews)   4'

Das Lied im Grünen, D917
(orch. Detlev Glanert)   5'

Beethoven
Overture 'Leonore' No. 3   13'

Angelika Kirchschlager mezzo-soprano

Apollo Voices (women's voices)
Gürzenich Orchestra
Markus Stenz conductor

When Mahler's Fifth Symphony was premiered in Cologne in October 1904, it shared a programme with Beethoven's *Leonore* No. 3 Overture and a group of Schubert songs. And it does so again this evening, though with a modern twist. The Schubert songs will be heard in contemporary orchestrations by four of today's leading composers, and nestling between the two 'original' halves, comes a performance of Stockhausen's *Punkte*, originally dating from almost exactly 50 years after the Mahler premiere (and also first heard in Cologne). It focuses on the opposition and resolution of six pairs of instruments. See *'Communing with the Cosmos', pages 28–31*

Spotlight on ... Markus Stenz

As the Gürzenich Orchestra marks 150 years of concert-giving in Cologne, it recreates at the Proms the concert of 1904 in which it introduced Mahler's Fifth Symphony to the world. And much to Music Director Markus Stenz's delight, his Prom with the orchestra inserts a work by Stockhausen into the mix, on the very day that Stockhausen would have turned 80.

'I love programmes with cross-references across more than one chapter of music,' says Stenz, 'and in this concert we can reflect not only our orchestra's tradition – by returning to a work that has become part of our history – but also the constantly evolving musical world. To add a further, fresh element, we have approached four composers to make these arrangements of Schubert songs. The Gürzenich Orchestra has always been known to play new pieces, so we're continuing that tradition.' *Punkte*, Stenz believes, will form 'a wonderful palate-cleanser' between works that have now become staples of the Austro-German repertoire.

Broadcast
RADIO Live on Radio 3
ONLINE Live and 'listen again' options at bbc.co.uk/proms

SATURDAY 23 AUGUST

Proms Plus 4.45pm, Royal College of Music
Family Music Intro Join some of the sensational young musicians from the NYO to discover the sound-worlds of Varèse, Rachmaninov and Copland. Bring your instrument and join in.
Free to ticket-holders

6.30pm–c8.45pm, Royal Albert Hall

Varèse
Amériques   24'

Rachmaninov
Piano Concerto No. 4 in G minor   26'

interval

Copland
Symphony No. 3   43'

Boris Berezovsky piano

National Youth Orchestra of Great Britain
Antonio Pappano conductor

A trio of works from America. Copland's great Third Symphony – with its portrayal of the wide, open spaces of North America – includes a striking reprise of the classic *Fanfare for the Common Man* at the start of the last movement. The symphony dates from the end of the Second World War and captures something of the sense of optimism of the American people at the time. From 25 years earlier, though sounding far more recent, comes Edgard Varèse's *Amériques*, whose title, he claimed, was 'symbolic of discoveries, of new worlds on Earth, in the sky or in the minds of men'; the first work that the Frenchman completed after arriving in New York, this still strikingly original score was premiered in Philadelphia by Leopold Stokowski. So too was Rachmaninov's Fourth (and last) Piano Concerto, also composed in the USA, where the composer had settled after leaving Russia in 1917. Rachmaninov himself was the soloist at the 1927 premiere; tonight it's the fearlessly virtuosic Boris Berezovsky. See *'A New Encounter', pages 34–35*

Broadcast
RADIO Live on Radio 3
ONLINE Live and 'listen again' options at bbc.co.uk/proms
TV Broadcast at 7.00pm on BBC Two

SUNDAY 24 AUGUST – BACH DAY

Proms Plus 1.00pm, Royal College of Music
Film *O Thou Transcendent* (148'). Tony Palmer's new biopic of Vaughan Williams, the first full-length documentary on the composer. Introduced by the director.
Free to all

Proms Plus 5.15pm, Royal College of Music
Proms Intro Sir John Eliot Gardiner and Mark Padmore discuss Bach's *St John Passion* with Christopher Cook.

Free to ticket-holders. Edited version will be available at bbc.co.uk/proms

10.00pm–c11.15pm, Royal Albert Hall

J. S. Bach
Suite No. 1 in G major for solo cello   *19'*
Suite No. 2 in D minor for solo cello   *23'*
Suite No. 3 in C major for solo cello   *24'*

Jian Wang *cello*

4.00pm–c5.00pm, Royal Albert Hall

J. S. Bach
Toccata and Fugue in D minor, BWV 565   *9'*

Canonic Variations on 'Vom Himmel Hoch', BWV 769   *11'*

Prelude and Fugue in E flat major, 'St Anne', BWV 552   *15'*

Chorale Prelude on 'Vater unser im Himmelreich', BWV 682   *7'*

Chorale Prelude on 'Aus tiefer Not schrei ich zu dir', BWV 687   *7'*

Duetto No. 2 in F major, BWV 803   *3'*

Simon Preston *organ*

Renowned Bach interpreter Simon Preston launches the Proms Bach Day, putting the Royal Albert Hall's recently restored Henry Willis organ through its paces.

There will be no interval

The Royal Albert Hall's Henry Willis organ

7.00pm–c9.10pm, Royal Albert Hall

J. S. Bach
St John Passion   *116'*

Mark Padmore *Evangelist*
Peter Harvey *Christus*
Katherine Fuge *soprano*
Robin Blaze *counter-tenor*
Nicholas Mulroy, Jeremy Budd *tenors*
Matthew Brook *bass*

Monteverdi Choir
English Baroque Soloists
Sir John Eliot Gardiner *conductor*

Sir John Eliot Gardiner, whose recordings of Bach have set new standards in interpretation, has said that 'if the *St Matthew Passion* begs comparison with some of Rembrandt's canvases, the *St John* is perhaps more like a Caravaggio: shafts of light in the gloom illuminating the key players in this most universal of stories'. It's a work that focuses on Jesus the man, and his confrontation with Pontius Pilate, with a dramatic insight that makes one regret the absence of a Bach opera. Mark Padmore, a regular collaborator with Gardiner, sings the Evangelist and Peter Harvey takes the part of Jesus. And weaving together the story of the Passion is the magnificent Monteverdi Choir.

There will be no interval

Jian Wang

Chinese cellist Jian Wang takes the stage of the Royal Albert Hall for the first three of Bach's six solo suites, works of towering technical accomplishment as well as intellectual and spiritual nourishment. Jiang Wang comments that 'Bach's music has a lot of qualities that appeal to the Chinese philosophy of life: to be humble, to wish but not desire, to love but not own. This is all in Chinese philosophy, and because I grew up with those values, these things are dear to me. When I listen to Bach's music, it confirms all of that.'

There will be no interval

SAME-DAY SAVER
Book for Proms 50, 51 and 52 and save (see page 136)

SAME-DAY SAVER
Book for Proms 50, 51 and 52 and save (see page 136)

Broadcast
RADIO Live on Radio 3
ONLINE Live and 'listen again' options at bbc.co.uk/proms

Broadcast
RADIO Live on Radio 3
ONLINE Live and 'listen again' options at bbc.co.uk/proms
TV Broadcast at 7.30pm on BBC Four

Broadcast
RADIO Live on Radio 3
ONLINE Live and 'listen again' options at bbc.co.uk/proms

MONDAY 25 AUGUST

X

1.00pm–c2.00pm

Proms Chamber Music at Cadogan Hall

Lambert
Air 'Vos mépris chaque jour' *4'*

Marais
Sonate à la marésienne – excerpts *8'*

Montéclair
Cantata 'Le dépit généreux' *14'*

Couperin
14è ordre – Le rossignol-en-amour;
Double du rossignol *10'*

Rameau
Cantata 'Orphée' *6'*

Les Talens Lyriques
Céline Scheen *soprano*
Stéphanie Paulet *violin*
Atsushi Sakaï *cello*
Christophe Rousset *harpsichord/director*

Christophe Rousset and friends focus on the French Baroque solo cantata – 'the heart's outpourings', as he describes it. 'I wanted to return to the essence of French Baroque music,' he says, and the eloquent cantatas by Montéclair and Rameau reflect the intimacy of chamber-music evenings at the court of Versailles. There's also a touching *air de cour* by Michel Lambert, and Couperin Le Grand's depictions of a nightingale.

Christophe Rousset

There will be no interval

Broadcast
RADIO Live on Radio 3
ONLINE Live and 'listen again' options at bbc.co.uk/proms

MONDAY 25 AUGUST

P/L

Proms Plus Royal College of Music (except 4.00pm)
11.30am Proms Family Orchestra A special extended Family Orchestra event. Join us to rehearse a new piece specially commissioned from Errollyn Wallen and perform in its world premiere at the RAH at 4.00pm (see page 67 for details).
1.00pm Film *Scott of the Antarctic* (106').
Introduced by Anthony Payne
4.00pm Proms Family Orchestra performs at the RAH
5.15pm Proms Literary Festival with children's authors Michael Morpurgo and Julian Donaldson
All events free to all. Ticket required for Literary Festival, available on the day at the RAH Box Office until 4.15pm and then on the door at the RCM. Edited broadcast of Literary Festival on Radio 3 during tonight's interval.

7.00pm–c9.10pm, Royal Albert Hall

Prokofiev
Romeo and Juliet – excerpts *45'*

interval

Tchaikovsky
Symphony No. 5 in E minor *48'*

Royal Philharmonic Orchestra
Daniele Gatti *conductor*

Two Russian masterpieces, both of them by composers fêted for their ballets as well as their symphonies. Daniele Gatti and his Royal Philharmonic Orchestra offer a selection from Prokofiev's amazingly original and thrilling music for *Romeo and Juliet*. They end with Tchaikovsky's great Fifth Symphony, in many ways as harrowing a work as the devastating *Pathétique* (Prom 66). Gatti's flair for orchestral colour and emotional intensity is well-suited to this Romantic idiom.

Broadcast
RADIO Live on Radio 3
ONLINE Live and 'listen again' options at bbc.co.uk/proms
TV Broadcast at 7.30pm on BBC Four

TUESDAY 26 AUGUST

P

Proms Plus 5.45pm, Royal College of Music
Proms Intro RCM Chief and Deputy Librarians, Pam Thompson and Peter Horton, join Michael Kennedy and Stephen Johnson to discuss Ralph Vaughan Williams on the 50th anniversary of his death
Free to ticket-holders. Edited version will be available at bbc.co.uk/proms

---

7.30pm–c10.05pm, Royal Albert Hall

Vaughan Williams
Fantasia on a Theme by Thomas Tallis *16'*

Job: A Masque for Dancing *44'*

interval

Serenade to Music *11'*

Symphony No. 9 in E minor *36'*

Sarah Tynan, Elizabeth Atherton, Sophie Bevan, Rachel Nicholls *sopranos*
Allison Cook, Louise Poole, Julia Riley, Catherine Hopper *mezzo-sopranos*
Ed Lyon, Joshua Ellicott, Peter Wedd, Nicholas Sharratt *tenors*
Mark Stone, Darren Jeffery, George von Bergen, Tim Mirfin *basses*

BBC Symphony Orchestra
Sir Andrew Davis *conductor*

A high point of our tribute to Vaughan Williams, who died 50 years ago today. Sir Andrew Davis, Conductor Laureate of the BBC SO, returns for a programme that opens with the much-loved *Fantasia on a Theme by Thomas Tallis*. Its rich, string-dominated textures are followed by the ballet, *Job*, first staged by Ninette de Valois. The *Serenade to Music*, to words by Shakespeare, was written for 16 leading British singers of the day and premiered by Henry Wood at his Jubilee Concert 70 years ago. And, to close, VW's last symphony, originally conceived as a programmatic work based on Thomas Hardy's *Tess of the d'Urbervilles*. See 'Two-Way Vision', pages 12–17

Broadcast
RADIO Live on Radio 3
ONLINE Live and 'listen again' options at bbc.co.uk/proms
TV Recorded for broadcast on BBC Two on 30 August (except *Job*).

WEDNESDAY 27 AUGUST

Proms Plus 5.15pm, Royal College of Music
Family Music Intro Bring your family to hear an introduction
to the stories behind tonight's music. Bring your instrument along
and take part.
Free to ticket-holders

7.00pm–c9.05pm, Royal Albert Hall

Debussy
Prélude à L'après-midi d'un faune   *10'*

Vaughan Williams
The Lark Ascending   *14'*

Peter Eötvös
Seven   *22'*
UK premiere

interval

Ravel
Shéhérazade   *18'*

Daphnis et Chloé – Suite No. 2   *17'*

Akiko Suwanai *violin*
Sarah Connolly *mezzo-soprano*

Philharmonia Orchestra
Peter Eötvös *conductor*

A programme with leanings towards the natural
world. Debussy's faun slumbers languidly in the heat
of a Mediterranean afternoon and Vaughan Williams's
lark climbs ever higher into the sky above England.
VW's teacher Maurice Ravel sets his ballet *Daphnis et
Chloé* in an Ancient Greece ravishingly lit by a sun that
dawns magnificently at the opening of the Second
Suite. And an Orient of sensuality and danger is
portrayed in the exotic song-cycle *Shéhérazade*.
Tonight's conductor introduces his own violin
concerto, *Seven*, to UK audiences, a work
written to commemorate the seven
astronauts who lost their lives in the space
shuttle *Columbia*. See 'Two-Way Vision', pages
12–17; 'New Music', pages 42–49

Broadcast
RADIO Live on Radio 3
ONLINE Live and 'listen again' options at bbc.co.uk/proms

WEDNESDAY 27 AUGUST

Proms Plus 9.15pm, Royal College of Music
Proms Literary Festival Ian McMillan explores literature
inspired by birds, with poet Katrina Porteous and nature writer
Mark Cocker. Free to all, ticket required, available on the day at the RAH
Box Office until 9.00pm and then on the door at the RCM. Edited
broadcast on Radio 3 on 28 August

10.00pm–c11.20pm, Royal Albert Hall

Einojuhani Rautavaara
Cantus arcticus   *18'*

Sir John Tavener
Cantus mysticus   *7'*
UK premiere

The Whale   *35'*

Patricia Rozario *soprano*
Susan Bickley *mezzo-soprano*
David Wilson-Johnson *baritone*
Mark van de Wiel *clarinet*

London Sinfonietta Chorus
London Sinfonietta
David Atherton *conductor*

Patricia Rozario

SAME-DAY SAVER
Book for both
Proms 55 and 56
and save (see
page 136)

The natural world of this evening's earlier Prom spills
over into this late-night London Sinfonietta concert.
Einojuhani Rautavaara's most popular work, a concerto
for taped birds and orchestra, marks the composer's
80th anniversary. And Sir John Tavener's early cantata
The Whale is heard again under the baton of David
Atherton, who gave its premiere at the London
Sinfonietta's inaugural concert 40 years ago. The
work was famously recorded on the Beatles' own
Apple label after Ringo Starr heard it. Forty years on,
Tavener offers the UK premiere of *Cantus mysticus*,
for soprano, clarinet and strings, with sets texts
by Goethe, Dante and others, concerned with the
creative Feminine element in the Divine. *See 'New
Music', pages 42–49*

There will be no interval

Broadcast
RADIO Live on Radio 3
ONLINE Live and 'listen again' options at bbc.co.uk/proms

Spotlight on ... Einojuhani Rautavaara

"I was composing a cantata
for the University of Oulu
[northern Finland], the 'Arctic
University', when the conductor
called to warn me that his
chorus was not in the best
shape. Could I refrain from
writing anything very tricky for
them, he asked. So there and
then I thought, 'I won't need your chorus, I'll write
the cantata for birds.'

Having spent my childhood summers in the
north, I knew that during the spring the swamps
and bogs would be filled with all kinds of birds,
including masses of migrating swans; so I travelled
there to tape their songs. At the time [1972] I was
very interested in electronics and so it seemed
natural to use tape too. I remember in the first
performance, in Helsinki, the tape recorder
obstinately refused to start, and I walked out
of the Finlandia Hall, creating a scandal!"

WEEKEND PROMMING PASS – BEAT THE QUEUES AND SAVE MONEY (SEE PAGE 136)

THURSDAY 28 AUGUST

Proms Plus 5.45pm, Royal College of Music
Proms Composer Portrait Steven Stucky, in conversation with Andrew McGregor, discusses his new Proms commission and introduces performances of some of his chamber works.
Free to all. Edited broadcast on Radio 3 later this evening

7.30pm–c9.35pm, Royal Albert Hall

Steven Stucky
Rhapsodies c12'
*BBC/New York Philharmonic
co-commission: world premiere*

Gershwin
Piano Concerto in F major 33'

interval

Stravinsky
The Rite of Spring 34'

Jean-Yves Thibaudet *piano*

New York Philharmonic
Lorin Maazel *conductor*

For the first of its two concerts, the New York Philharmonic unveils a joint commission with the BBC by the Pulitzer Prize-winning composer Steven Stucky. 'Rhapsodies,' Stucky writes, features 'successive waves of ecstatic, extravagant expression that ripple outward from a single soloist until they involve whole sections of the orchestra. In this way it celebrates the brilliance of the New York Philharmonic musicians, both singly and collectively.' Proms regular Jean-Yves Thibaudet is the soloist in Gershwin's Piano Concero – every bit as toe-tapping and scintillating as his *Rhapsody in Blue*, completed the previous year. Lorin Maazel also conducts Stravinsky's great ballet score *The Rite of Spring*, an exploration of primeval Russian ritual – as shocking now as it was nearly a century ago at its riotous Paris premiere. See 'New Music', pages 42–49

Broadcast
RADIO Live on Radio 3
ONLINE Live and 'listen again' options at bbc.co.uk/proms

FRIDAY 29 AUGUST

Proms Plus 5.45pm, Royal College of Music
Proms Intro Join Zarin Mehta, New York Philharmonic President and Executive Director, and musicians from the orchestra in an exploration of the Philharmonic's musical and educational activities
Free to ticket-holders. Edited version will be available at bbc.co.uk/proms

7.30pm–c9.35pm, Royal Albert Hall

Ravel
Mother Goose – suite 19'

Bartók
The Miraculous Mandarin – suite 20'

interval

Tchaikovsky
Symphony No. 4 in F minor 43'

New York Philharmonic
Lorin Maazel *conductor*

Lorin Maazel

The New York Philharmonic and its music director Lorin Maazel contrast two early 20th-century scores of abundant colour with one of the greatest Russian symphonies. Ravel orchestrated his *Mother Goose* suite from a piano-duet original, creating a kaleidoscope of sound, and Bartók drew his *Miraculous Mandarin* suite from his somewhat ghoulish ballet score – and once again proved what a master of the orchestra he was, able to send a shudder up the spine at will. Tchaikovsky's powerful Fourth Symphony, written at the time of his disastrous agreement to marry an over-zealous admirer, presents Fate as 'the force of destiny, which ever prevents our pursuit of happiness from reaching its goal'.

Broadcast
RADIO Live on Radio 3
ONLINE Live and 'listen again' options at bbc.co.uk/proms

SATURDAY 30 AUGUST

Proms Plus Royal College of Music
2.00pm **Proms Family Orchestra** Free (see page 67)
5.45pm **Proms Literary Festival** BBC Diplomatic Correspondent Bridget Kendall on Russian literature and current affairs.
Free to ticket-holders. Literature Festival edited version will be available at bbc.co.uk/proms

7.30pm–c10.05pm, Royal Albert Hall

Magnus Lindberg
Seht die Sonne 29'
UK premiere

Rachmaninov
Piano Concerto No. 3 in D minor 43'

interval

Sibelius
Symphony No. 1 in E minor 38'

Nikolai Lugansky *piano*

Oslo Philharmonic Orchestra
Jukka-Pekka Saraste *conductor*

Nikolai Lugansky

Jukka-Pekka Saraste and the Oslo Philharmonic bring two Finnish works as well as one of the greatest of all Russian piano concertos. Finnish composer Magnus Lindberg's *Seht die Sonne* was commissioned jointly by the Berliner Philharmoniker and the San Francisco Symphony, and unveiled under the baton of Sir Simon Rattle in Berlin last year. Taking its title from the last chorus in Schoenberg's *Gurrelieder*, it was written for the same scale of forces as for that pinnacle of Viennese High Romanticism, Mahler's Ninth Symphony. Sibelius's First was his most Russian symphony, with a touch of Tchaikovsky in its language, but evidently the work of a master symphonist in the making. See 'A New Encounter', pages 34–35; 'New Music', 42–49

Broadcast
RADIO Live on Radio 3
ONLINE Live and 'listen again' options at bbc.co.uk/proms

SUNDAY 31 AUGUST

Proms Plus 2.15pm, Royal College of Music
Family Music Intro Discover the incredible world of the piano
– its many styles, sounds and techniques – in this special Music
Intro event dedicated to this dazzlingly versatile instrument.
Free to ticket-holders

4.00pm–c5.30pm, Royal Albert Hall

Mozart
Piano Sonata *(to be announced)*   c20'

Rachmaninov
Preludes – selection   c9'

Debussy
Préludes – selection   c8'

Schubert
Fantasia in F minor, D940*   18'

Chopin
Andante spianato et Grande Polonaise
brillante, Op. 22   14'

Waltzes – selection   c6'

Liszt
Hungarian Rhapsody No. 2   10'

Lang Lang *piano*
with **Marc Yu** * *piano*

One of the few genuine classical superstars, as
popular in the West as in his native China, Lang Lang
attracts loyal audiences around the world with his
high-octane pianism. This family-friendly recital for the
bank holiday weekend features some of the composers
he has especially favoured during his career so far –
and a duet performance with the 9-year-old pianist
he has dubbed 'little Mozart', Marc Yu. See 'A New
Encounter', pages 34–35

There will be no interval

Broadcast
RADIO Live on Radio 3
ONLINE Live and 'listen again' options at bbc.co.uk/proms
TV Broadcast at 7.30pm on BBC Four

Spotlight on ... Lang Lang

This year young Chinese-born Lang Lang makes
his fourth appearance at the Proms, this time to
give a solo piano recital. And in one item,
Schubert's Fantasia in F minor, he will share the
keyboard with 9-year-old, California-born Marc Yu,
for whom Lang Lang was only a distant idol until
they first met. 'I met Marc through a friend in the
TV world,' explains Lang Lang, 'who told me that
this kid was really something rare. And so I met
him and he played for me. He has a very special
talent and he's also a wonderful, sweet kid.'

   Though himself only in his mid-twenties,
Lang Lang has been appearing at the leading
international venues and festivals for several
years, having made his debut with the Chicago
Symphony Orchestra aged 17. He keenly looks
forward to returning to the Proms. 'I made
my London concerto debut at the Proms
in 2001, and I just find it to be the most
exciting place to perform on Earth. The
audience is so attentive, and with the Prommers
standing it's a little like being at a rock concert.
I can't wait to feel the power from the audience.
For a performer, it is the most powerful
experience you can get.'

**SAME-
DAY SAVER**
Book for both
Proms 60 and 61
and save (see
page 136)

SUNDAY 31 AUGUST

Proms Plus 6.15pm, Royal College of Music
Proms Intro Join Suzy Klein, Roger Parker and Susan Rutherford
in this introduction to one of the best-known choral works in the
repertory – Verdi's *Requiem*.
Free to ticket-holders. Edited version will be available at bbc.co.uk/proms

8.00pm–c9.35pm, Royal Albert Hall

Verdi
Requiem   85'

Violeta Urmana *soprano*
Olga Borodina *mezzo-soprano*
Joseph Calleja *tenor*
Ildebrando d'Arcangelo *bass*

BBC Symphony Chorus
Crouch End Festival Chorus
BBC Symphony Orchestra
Jiří Bělohlávek *conductor*

In May 1875 London experienced the first British
performance of Verdi's *Requiem* – in the Royal Albert
Hall, with Verdi conducting. The reception was
tumultuous and the press reviews spoke of the work
in the same breath as of Mozart's hallowed *Requiem*.
Written in memory of the great Italian writer
Alessandro Manzoni, Verdi's Mass for the dead –
a work controversially composed by an atheist –
has become as popular as his operas. The composer
regarded it is as one of his greatest achievements:
'I feel as if I have become a serious citizen, and am no
longer the public's clown.' A stellar international line-up
of soloists and massed choirs join the BBC Symphony
Orchestra and its Chief Conductor Jiří Bělohlávek for
a work vividly coloured by Verdi's dramatic instinct.

There will be no interval

Broadcast
RADIO Live on Radio 3
ONLINE Live and 'listen again' options at bbc.co.uk/proms

MONDAY I SEPTEMBER ∟

1.00pm–c2.00pm

Proms Chamber Music at Cadogan Hall

Coleridge-Taylor
Clarinet Quintet *35'*

Vaughan Williams
On Wenlock Edge *23'*

Mark Padmore *tenor*
Nash Ensemble

Mark Padmore

Mark Padmore makes his second Proms appearance this year, in Vaughan Williams's moving *On Wenlock Edge* (see also Prom 51). The song-cycle's six settings of words by A. E. Housman form a touching exploration of hope and loss. The Clarinet Quintet by Samuel Coleridge-Taylor – a fellow student of Vaughan Williams at the Royal College of Music – was written following a challenge to the composer by his teacher, Stanford, to write a work that would match up to Brahms's famous Clarinet Quintet. He succeeded admirably, crafting a work of heartfelt lyricism and charm. See *'Two-Way Vision', pages 12–17*

There will be no interval

Broadcast
RADIO Live on Radio 3
ONLINE Live and 'listen again' options at bbc.co.uk/proms

MONDAY I SEPTEMBER ✗

Proms Plus 5.15pm, Royal College of Music
Family Music Intro Bring your instrument along for a chance to join members of the Gustav Mahler Jugendorchester and discover more about tonight's music.
Free to ticket-holders

7.00pm–c9.10pm, Royal Albert Hall

Beethoven
Violin Concerto in D major *45'*

interval

Sibelius
Symphony No. 2 in D major *45'*

Nikolaj Znaider *violin*

Gustav Mahler Jugendorchester
Sir Colin Davis *conductor*

A dynamic young soloist – born in Denmark to Polish-Israeli parents – joins tonight's great pan-European youth orchestra for Beethoven's only violin concerto. Znaider views this work as the violinist's 'bible', its 'ultimate challenge' – and in his musical partners he can rely on the freshness of youth coupled with Sir Colin's wisdom and experience. Davis ends the concert with a work he understands like few of his colleagues, Sibelius's Second, first heard in 1902. 'The effect of the Andante,' wrote the great Finnish conductor Robert Kajanus, 'is that of the most crushing protest against all the injustice which today threatens to take light from the sun.'

Broadcast
RADIO Live on Radio 3
ONLINE Live and 'listen again' options at bbc.co.uk/proms
TV Broadcast at 7.30pm on BBC Four. Violin Concerto also recorded for broadcast on BBC Two on 6 September.

MONDAY I SEPTEMBER ∟

10.00pm–c11.30pm, Royal Albert Hall

Motets and chansons by **Claude Le Jeune**, **Antoine Brumel** and **Claudin de Sermisy**, interspersed with Indian ragas *c15*

Messiaen
Cinq rechants *20'*

Night ragas *c45'*

Nishat Khan *sitar*
Rashid Mustafa Thirakwa *tabla*
Emmanuel Masongsong *tanpura*

BBC Singers
David Hill *conductor*

The Proms' Messiaen centenary celebrations continue with *Cinq rechants* (the second instalment of the composer's Tristan trilogy – see PCM 4 and Prom 64), which draws its inspiration from Sanskrit texts, traditional Indian rhythms and Renaissance polyphony. Tonight's opening sequence likewise weaves together music of the East and West. Nishat Khan (known for his imaginative fusions of European and Asian musical traditions) joins the BBC Singers in a sequence of French Renaissance chansons and motets (exploring the season of spring and the erotic imagery associated with it) woven around improvised classical Indian ragas for similar times, seasons and states of mind, to create a sensual sound-world which echoes that of Messiaen. Khan concludes with a selection of night ragas, chosen according to the mood of the occasion. See *'The Light of Sound', pages 20–25*

There will be no interval

SAME-DAY SAVER Book for both Proms 62 and 63 and save (see page 136)

Nishat Khan

Broadcast
RADIO Live on Radio 3
ONLINE Live and 'listen again' options at bbc.co.uk/proms

TUESDAY 2 SEPTEMBER L

Proms Plus 5.45pm, Royal College of Music
Proms Intro Martin Handley talks to Tristan Murail about the ondes martenot, and this intriguing electronic instrument's role in Messiaen's *Turangalîla Symphony*.
Free to ticket-holders. Edited version will be available at bbc.co.uk/proms

---

7.30pm–c9.40pm, Royal Albert Hall

Wagner
Tristan und Isolde – Prelude and Liebestod 18'

interval

Messiaen
Turangalîla Symphony 78'

Pierre-Laurent Aimard *piano*
Tristan Murail *ondes martenot*

Berliner Philharmoniker
Sir Simon Rattle *conductor*

The story of Tristan and Isolde inspires tonight's Prom by the great Berliner Philharmoniker and its Principal Conductor, Sir Simon Rattle. The concert opens with the powerful pairing from either end of Wagner's great opera of love and death – its opening notes fused with the concluding 'love-death' of its heroine. Then pianist Pierre-Laurent Aimard, in the last of his three appearances this year (see Prom 1 and PCM 1) and ondes martenot player Tristan Murail join the orchestra for Messiaen's ecstatic *Turangalîla Symphony* – the central apex of the French composer's Tristan trilogy. It's a work whose rhythmic complexity has been within Rattle's firm grasp for over 20 years. And, as the conductor has declared, 'If rhythm is primarily an expression of the life-force, who better to be our guide than Olivier Messiaen?' *See 'The Light of Sound', pages 20–25*

Broadcast
RADIO Live on Radio 3
ONLINE Live and 'listen again' options at bbc.co.uk/proms

WEDNESDAY 3 SEPTEMBER X

Proms Plus 5.30pm, Royal College of Music
Family Music Intro Find out more about Brahms and Shostakovich, plus a look at the Berliner Philharmoniker's education programme and a showcase of a recent project on Brahms.
Free to ticket-holders

7.30pm–c9.40pm, Royal Albert Hall

Brahms
Symphony No. 3 in F major 35'

interval

Shostakovich
Symphony No. 10 in E minor 54'

Berliner Philharmoniker
Sir Simon Rattle *conductor*

Sir Simon Rattle and his Berlin orchestra open their second Prom of the season with a work central to the ensemble's repertoire: Brahms's Symphony No. 3, the mellowest of his four symphonies, inspired by a visit to the Rhine in 1883. Seventy years later came Shostakovich's powerful Tenth Symphony, written just months after the death of Stalin. Its long opening movement seems to sum up the suffering of Shostakovich and his compatriots under Stalin's regime, and it's hard not to hear a note of triumph when Shostakovich's motto signature DSCH appears in the finale.

Sir Simon Rattle

Broadcast
RADIO Live on Radio 3
ONLINE Live and 'listen again' options at bbc.co.uk/proms
TV Recorded for broadcast on BBC Four on 7 September

THURSDAY 4 SEPTEMBER P

Proms Plus 5.15pm, Royal College of Music
Proms Literary Festival Ian McMillan introduces writing about the sea with poets John Agard – who has recently been working with the National Maritime Museum – and Jean Sprackland.
Free to ticket-holders. Edited broadcast on Radio 3 on 6 September

---

7.00pm–c9.10pm, Royal Albert Hall

Grace Williams
Sea Sketches 19'

Elgar
Sea Pictures 23'

interval

Tchaikovsky
Symphony No. 6, 'Pathétique' 49'

Christine Rice *mezzo-soprano*

BBC National Orchestra of Wales
Tadaaki Otaka *conductor*

The sea dominates the first half of this BBC NOW Prom. A pupil of Vaughan Williams, Grace Williams showed a debt in her musical language to her teacher (with perhaps a sideways glance at Elgar). Her *Sea Sketches*, a five-movement work for strings, dates from the Second World War and makes a perfect companion to Elgar's glorious settings of his wife's poetry in *Sea Pictures* – songs of an almost rapturous abandon, sung tonight by former Radio 3 New Generation Artist Christine Rice. Tadaaki Otaka, the BBC National Orchestra of Wales's Conductor Laureate, closes the concert with Tchaikovsky's last symphony, a work premiered just nine days before the death of the composer, who claimed: 'Without exaggeration, I have put my whole soul into it.'

SAME DAY SAVER
Book for both Proms 66 and 67 and save (see page 136)

Broadcast
RADIO Live on Radio 3
ONLINE Live and 'listen again' options at bbc.co.uk/proms

THURSDAY 4 SEPTEMBER *P/L*

10.00pm–c11.00pm, Royal Albert Hall

Messiaen
Quartet for the End of Time *50'*

Martin Fröst clarinet
Anthony Marwood violin
Matthew Barley cello
Thomas Larcher piano

Martin Fröst

A late-night opportunity to hear one of the most luminous chamber works of the 20th century. Olivier Messiaen was a prisoner of war in a German camp, Stalag VIII-A in Görlitz (now Zgorzelec, Poland), and – encountering a clarinettist, violinist and cellist there – he set about writing a work for them, with himself in mind as pianist. The resulting *Quartet for the End of Time* was first heard on 15 January 1941 before a huge audience of prisoners and prison guards. 'Never was I listened to with such rapt attention and comprehension,' Messiaen later said. Four of today's finest young musicians come together to perform this extraordinary work. Martin Fröst returns for his second performance of the season, having performed Anders Hillborg's clarinet concerto in Prom 37.
See 'The Light of Sound', pages 20–25

SAME-DAY SAVER Book for both Proms 66 and 67 and save (see page 136)

Broadcast
RADIO Live on Radio 3
ONLINE Live and 'listen again' options at bbc.co.uk/proms

FRIDAY 5 SEPTEMBER *L*

WEEKEND PROMMING PASS – BEAT THE QUEUES AND SAVE MONEY (SEE PAGE 136)

Proms Plus 5.45pm, Royal College of Music
Proms Literary Festival Susan Hitch explores the world of Russian fairy tales with Moscow-born writer Zinovy Zinik and Robert Chandler, who is editing a new anthology.
Free to ticket-holders. Edited broadcast on Radio 3 during tonight's interval

7.30pm–c9.55pm, Royal Albert Hall

Rimsky-Korsakov
Kashchey the Immortal *(concert performance; sung in Russian)* *60'*

interval

Stravinsky
The Firebird *46'*

Vyacheslav Voynarovsky *Kashchey*
Tatiana Monogarova *Princess*
Pavel Baransky *Ivan Korolevich*
Elena Manistina *Kashcheyevna*
Mikhail Petrenko *Storm Knight*

BBC Singers
London Philharmonic Orchestra
Vladimir Jurowski conductor

Vladimir Jurowski

Marking the centenary of Rimsky-Korsakov's death (see also Prom 35), and concluding a trio of short operas at this year's Proms (see also Proms 34 & 47), Vladimir Jurowski conducts the Russian composer's rarely heard opera about the evil wizard Kashchey. In the second half comes the ballet that Rimsky-Korsakov's pupil Igor Stravinsky wrote eight years later for Diaghilev's Ballets Russes, which also enters into Kashchey's magical realm.

Broadcast
RADIO Live on Radio 3
ONLINE Live and 'listen again' options at bbc.co.uk/proms

Spotlight on ... Tatiana Monogarova

Born in Moscow, soprano Tatiana Monogarova has a natural affinity with the tale on which Rimsky's opera *Kashchey the Immortal* – and also Stravinsky's well-known ballet *The Firebird* – is based. 'Every child in Russia,' she says, 'knows the fairy tale. There is a cartoon based on the story and also a painting by Viktor Vasnetsov, which is a work of great beauty. The role of the beautiful Princess has an underlying current based on folk singing. Her lonely lament, a melody full of grief and sorrow which intertwines with the harmonies, is drawn out to the fullest effect.' Fellow Russian Vladimir Jurowski – Principal Conductor of the London Philharmonic Orchestra and also Music Director of Glyndebourne Festival Opera – is the ideal person for the podium. 'I always look forward to collaborations with him with joy and impatience,' enthuses the soprano. 'Every project on which we have worked together has been characterised by a mixture of trust, searching, agreement, inspiration and creativity.'

WEEKEND PROMMING PASS – BEAT THE QUEUES AND SAVE MONEY (SEE PAGE 136)

SATURDAY 6 SEPTEMBER

Proms Plus 5.45pm, Royal College of Music
Proms Literary Festival TV dramatist Stephen Poliakoff joins Susan Hitch to talk about his favourite Russian literature and its influence on his work.
Free to ticket-holders. Edited broadcast on Radio 3 on 9 September

7.30pm–c9.45pm, Royal Albert Hall

Roussel
Bacchus et Ariane – Suite No. 2   20'

Rachmaninov
Piano Concerto No. 2 in C minor   35'

interval

Thea Musgrave
Rainbow   12'

Debussy
La mer   24'

Stephen Hough piano

Royal Scottish National Orchestra
Stéphane Denève conductor

Stephen Hough

A nod in the direction of the Auld Alliance as the Royal Scottish National Orchestra and its acclaimed French Music Director return to the Proms. Roussel's colourful second suite from the ballet *Bacchus et Ariane* opens the concert. ('The RSNO's performance is fully alive to the music's irrepressible *joie de vivre* as well as its more lyrical aspects,' wrote *Gramophone* of the orchestra's first Roussel disc.) Debussy's symphonic sketches of the sea close the concert. In between come a vivid picture of a storm – first performed 18 years ago by tonight's orchestra – from Thea Musgrave (in her 80th-birthday year); and Rachmaninov's most popular piano concerto, featuring award-winning interpreter Stephen Hough. See 'A New Encounter', pages 34–35

Broadcast
RADIO Live on Radio 3
ONLINE Live and 'listen again' options at bbc.co.uk/proms

SUNDAY 7 SEPTEMBER

Proms Plus 2.15pm, Royal College of Music
Proms Intro Tom Service and Messiaen scholars Peter Hill and Nigel Simeone discuss Messiaen's *Saint Francis of Assisi*.
Free to ticket-holders. Edited broadcast on Radio 3 during tonight's first interval

4.00pm–c10.00pm, Royal Albert Hall

Messiaen
Saint Francis of Assisi
(concert performance; sung in French)   240'

The Netherlands Opera

Rod Gilfry *St Francis*
Heidi Grant Murphy *Angel*
Hubert Delamboye *Leper*
Henk Neven *Brother Leo*
Charles Workman *Brother Masseo*
Donald Kaasch *Brother Elias*
Armand Arapian *Brother Bernard*
Jan Willem Baljet *Brother Sylvester*
André Morsch *Brother Rufus*

Chorus of The Netherlands Opera
The Hague Philharmonic
Ingo Metzmacher conductor

Commissioned to write an opera by Rolf Liebermann for the Paris Opéra, Messiaen turned to the legend of St Francis of Assisi. It's a huge work with an entirely male cast, except for a single soprano in the role of the Angel. A keen ornithologist, Messiaen travelled to Assisi to listen to, and transcribe, the various calls and songs of the birds of the region – and he wove them into his score. In his last season as Chief Conductor of The Netherlands Opera, Ingo Metzmacher, a notable champion of 20th-century music, conducts a strong international cast drawn from director Pierre Audi's new Messiaen centenary production. See 'The Light of Sound', pages 20–25

There will be two intervals, of 20 and 60 minutes

Broadcast
RADIO Live on Radio 3
ONLINE Live and 'listen again' options at bbc.co.uk/proms

Spotlight on ... Ingo Metzmacher

"*Saint Francis of Assisi* is an exceptional opera. I don't know of any other composer after 1945 who would pick a religious subject and express his beliefs in such a huge piece. The music itself stuns me – it is so colourful and radiant. Unusually for an opera, too, it is not essentially dramatic; Messiaen was more interested in capturing the image of mountains and birds singing and mysteries beyond Earth. There are two scenes when the momentum of the music builds up, but even then, it's nothing like Verdi or Wagner! It has challenges for the conductor, because of its length – you have to have the physical strength to keep the music together for so long. However, it's not a difficult piece to listen to at all. You are struck by the beauty of the music right from the start, and once you get used to the slower passing of time and ease yourself into the ritual of the work, it is an overwhelming experience. I cannot compare it to many things I have encountered in music."

MONDAY 8 SEPTEMBER

1.00pm–c2.00pm

Proms Chamber Music at Cadogan Hall

R. Strauss
Capriccio – Sextet 12'

Fauré
La bonne chanson 24'

Huw Watkins
Sad Steps c15'
BBC commission: world premiere

Elizabeth Watts soprano
Aronowitz Ensemble

Elizabeth Watts

Richard Strauss's intimate and delicate string sextet from his last opera opens this final concert of the season's Proms Chamber Music series, given by some of the brightest of the current Radio 3 New Generation Artists. Elizabeth Watts (who returns in Prom 73) then sings Fauré's exquisitely beautiful song-cycle *La bonne chanson*. In this version with piano and string quintet, these settings of Verlaine take on an incandescent array of colours. Finally, a new work specially commissioned from Welsh composer Huw Watkins, with an evocative title suggested by a Philip Larkin poem. See 'New Music', pages 42–49

MONDAY 8 SEPTEMBER

Proms Plus 5.45pm, Royal College of Music
Composer Portrait Mark-Anthony Turnage, in conversation with Andrew McGregor, discusses his *Chicago Remains* and introduces performances of some of his chamber works.
Free to all. Edited broadcast on Radio 3 later this evening

7.30pm–c9.45pm, Royal Albert Hall

Mark-Anthony Turnage
Chicago Remains 16'
UK premiere

interval

Mahler
Symphony No. 6 in A minor 85'

Chicago Symphony Orchestra
Bernard Haitink conductor

Bernard Haitink

A welcome return to the Proms of the Chicago Symphony Orchestra, this time under its new Principal Conductor Bernard Haitink. *Chicago Remains* – by one of the CSO's Composers-in-Residence, Mark-Anthony Turnage – was inspired by the striking architecture of Chicago and the poetry of Carl Sandburg, but Turnage says he was also influenced by memories of the 1970s Bruckner recordings by Haitink (who gave the work's premiere last October). The title-page is inscribed to the memory of Sir John Drummond, a former Director of the BBC Proms and an early and loyal champion of Turnage's music. In the second half, Haitink conducts one of Mahler's greatest symphonies: a work of staggering power that seems to challenge Fate, but ultimately yields in the face of its overpowering force. See 'New Music', pages 42–49

TUESDAY 9 SEPTEMBER

Proms Plus 5.15pm, Royal College of Music
Film *Beyond the Score* Discover Shostakovich's Symphony No. 4; introduced by Martha Gilmer, Vice President for Artistic and Audience Development, Chicago Symphony Orchestra.
Free to ticket-holders

7.30pm–c9.45pm, Royal Albert Hall

Mozart
Piano Concerto No. 24 in C minor, K491 30'

interval

Shostakovich
Symphony No. 4 in C minor 67'

Murray Perahia piano

Chicago Symphony Orchestra
Bernard Haitink conductor

Murray Perahia and Bernard Haitink have a musical rapport that has given us countless magnificent performances. Tonight they are reunited – as Perahia returns to the Proms following a gap of 20 years – in one of Mozart's greatest piano concertos. It was while writing his Fourth Symphony that Shostakovich was denounced in an article entitled 'Muddle instead of music'. He continued composing in private, though the work had to wait 25 years – beyond the death of Stalin – before it was first heard, in 1961.

Murray Perahia

WEDNESDAY 10 SEPTEMBER

Proms Plus 4.45pm, Royal College of Music
Proms Literary Festival Ian McMillan gazes at the stars
and discusses planetary literature with poet Lavinia Greenlaw
and others.
Free to ticket-holders. Edited broadcast on Radio 3 during tonight's interval

6.30pm–c9.20pm, Royal Albert Hall

Vaughan Williams
Sinfonia antartica (Symphony No. 7) *42'*

interval

Xenakis
Pleiades *44'*

interval

Holst
The Planets *52'*

Elizabeth Watts soprano

4-Mality
O Duo
Holst Singers (women's voices)
BBC Symphony Orchestra
Martyn Brabbins conductor

One of the greatest – and most popular – of all
British orchestral works ends tonight's programme.
Martyn Brabbins conducts Holst's astrological suite,
The Planets, with the Holst Singers ushering us into
nothingness in the closing 'Neptune'. Iannis Xenakis's
Pleiades, too, looks to the skies. Scored for a sextet of
exotic percussion, *Pleiades* portrays, in the composer's
words, 'clouds, nebulas and galaxies of the fragmented
dust of beats organised by rhythm'. It's a work of great
drama, at times quite brutal, and drawing on Xenakis's
experiences in the Second World War during which
he lost the sight in one eye. Vaughan Williams's chilly
evocation of the vast, uninhabited wastes of the South
Pole opens the evening, with Elizabeth Watts (see
PCM 8) returning for the wordless soprano part.
See 'Two-Way Vision', pages 12–17

O Duo

Spotlight on ... Martyn Brabbins

Martyn Brabbins found the
idea of a programme linked
by the concept of frontiers and
exploration an immediately
appealing one. 'Everyone
knows Holst's suite as possibly
the most suggestive musical
representation of anything –
especially of anything quite
Martyn Brabbins

as extraordinary as the planets. And the Vaughan
Williams, while not astrologically related, is a very
spacious piece: its wonderful, cavernous sonorities
give that feeling of otherworldliness. In Xenakis's
Pleiades you can tell there's a rigorous mind
behind the organised, architectural structures,
but the response as a listener is a very direct,
physical one.' And just as *The Planets* recedes
into the ether with a celestial choir, so Vaughan
Williams's *Sinfonia antartica* ends, says Brabbins,
'with the vastness of nature magically subsuming
the human voice'.

Broadcast
RADIO Live on Radio 3
ONLINE Live and 'listen again' options at bbc.co.uk/proms

THURSDAY 11 SEPTEMBER

Proms Plus 5.45pm, Royal College of Music
Proms Intro Suzy Klein, Keith James and guests discuss the
influence of architecture in the music of Gustav Mahler.

Free to ticket-holders

7.30pm–c9.30pm, Royal Albert Hall

Matthias Pintscher
Hérodiade-Fragmente *22'*

interval

Mahler
Symphony No. 1 in D major *55'*

Marisol Montalvo soprano

Orchestre de Paris
Christoph Eschenbach conductor

Christoph Eschenbach
has long championed
the music of the German
composer Matthias
Pintscher, and tonight he
offers the Mallarmé-
inspired *Hérodiade-
Fragmente* – the piece for
soprano and orchestra
Marisol Montalvo

which Eschenbach was due to conduct here in 2006
with the Philadelphia Orchestra, before a small fire
at the Royal Albert Hall forced the concert to be
abandoned. Mahler's First Symphony opens magically
with the sounds of nature as it teems with life.
Eschenbach's Mahler has been widely admired, and
his galvanising effect on tonight's relatively young
orchestra (it was only founded in 1967) has been
one of the musical talking points of the French capital.

Marisol Montalvo

Broadcast
RADIO Live on Radio 3
ONLINE Live and 'listen again' options at bbc.co.uk/proms

FRIDAY 12 SEPTEMBER ✗

Proms Plus 5.45pm, Royal College of Music
Proms Intro Petroc Trelawny looks back on the 2008 Proms season, with Proms Director Roger Wright and Royal Albert Hall Chief Executive David Elliott.
Free to ticket-holders. Edited version will be available at bbc.co.uk/proms

---

7.30pm–c9.50pm, Royal Albert Hall

Wagner
Parsifal – Prelude (Act 1) *13'*

Krzysztof Penderecki
Threnody 'For the Victims of Hiroshima' *9'*

Beethoven
Elegischer Gesang *6'*

interval

Beethoven
Symphony No. 9 in D minor, 'Choral' *70'*

Emma Bell *soprano*
Jane Irwin *mezzo-soprano*
Timothy Robinson *tenor*
Iain Paterson *bass*

City of Birmingham Symphony Chorus
BBC Philharmonic
Gianandrea Noseda *conductor*

The traditional annual performance of Beethoven's 'Choral' Symphony falls to the BBC Philharmonic and Gianandrea Noseda, whose Beethoven cycle in 2005 won glowing plaudits. The spiritually shimmering Prelude to Act 1 of Wagner's opera *Parsifal* leads to Penderecki's moving memorial to the victims of Hiroshima, before Beethoven's rarely heard *Elegiac Song*, written in 1814 for a friend whose wife had died in childbirth. So in tonight's Prom it is from the emotional fallout of spiritual searching, then of man's inhumanity to man, and finally of a poignant, personal farewell that Beethoven's life-affirming Ninth Symphony rises, with the universal human message of its 'Ode to Joy'.

Broadcast
RADIO Live on Radio 3
ONLINE Live and 'listen again' options at bbc.co.uk/proms

SATURDAY 13 SEPTEMBER L

Proms Plus 5.30pm, Royal College of Music
Proms Intro Start your Last Night by joining others to sing favourite folk songs from the British Isles.

Free to ticket-holders.

8.00pm–c10.35pm, Royal Albert Hall

The Last Night of the Proms 2008

Beethoven
The Creatures of Prometheus – overture *6'*

Wagner
Tannhäuser – 'Wie Todesahnung Dämmrung … O du, mein holder Abendstern' (Act 3) *5'*

Puccini
Tosca – 'Tre sbirri, una carrozza' (Act 1, Te Deum) *4'*

Verdi
Falstaff – 'Ehi! paggio! … L'onore! Ladri!' (Act 1) *5'*

Beethoven
Fantasia in C minor for piano, chorus and orchestra, 'Choral Fantasy' *19'*

interval

Denza, arr. Rimsky-Korsakov
Funiculì, funiculà *3'*

Trad., arr. Britten
The Foggy, Foggy Dew (Suffolk Song) *3'*

Trad., arr. Chris Hazell
Folk Song Medley: The Turtle Dove (England) – Loch Lomond (Scotland) – Cariad cyntaf (Wales) – Molly Malone (Ireland) *c12'*
BBC commission: world premiere

Anna Meredith
new work *c5'*
BBC commission: world premiere

Elgar
Pomp and Circumstance March No. 1 *8'*

Vaughan Williams
Sea Songs *4'*

Arne, arr. Sargent
Rule, Britannia! *8'*

Parry, orch. Elgar
Jerusalem *2'*

The National Anthem *2'*

Bryn Terfel *bass-baritone*
Hélène Grimaud *piano*

BBC Singers
BBC Symphony Chorus
BBC Symphony Orchestra
Sir Roger Norrington *conductor*

Over 40 years since his Proms debut, Sir Roger Norrington makes his first Last Night appearance. In the first half, Bryn Terfel prays to the stars (as Wolfram in *Tannhäuser*), delivers his highly individual concept of honour (as Verdi's *Falstaff*) and renounces God in favour of Tosca (as Scarpia in *Tosca*) – and French pianist Hélène Grimaud appears in Beethoven's 'Choral' Fantasy (with pre-echoes of the Ninth Symphony's 'Ode to Joy'). The second-half festivities include Anna Meredith's nation-hopping commission as well as a final Vaughan Williams instalment, and a celebration of folk music – a central feature of VW's musical outlook – reflecting back on our earlier Proms Folk Day.
See 'New Music', pages 42–49

Hélène Grimaud

Bryn Terfel

Broadcast
RADIO Live on Radio 3
ONLINE Live and 'listen again' options at bbc.co.uk/proms
TV First half live on BBC Two. Second half live on BBC One

Kasskara/DG (Grimaud); Brian Tarr (Terfel)

The Last Night magic, live in the open air!

BBC PROMS IN THE PARK

Each of the four BBC Proms in the Park events, sponsored by National Savings and Investments, is centred around a live concert with high-profile artists and presenters, culminating in a live Big Screen link-up to the Royal Albert Hall. So gather together your friends, pack a picnic and get ready for a fabulous night out.

If there isn't a Proms in the Park event near to you, you can join the party at one of the BBC Big Screens around the country: Birmingham (Chamberlain Square), Bradford (Centenary Square), Derby (Market Place), Hull (Queen Victoria Square), Leeds (Millennium Square), Liverpool (Clayton Square), Manchester (Exchange Square), Rotherham (All Saints Square), Swindon (Wharf Green) and other new screens currently being commissioned across the UK.

This year's concerts are broadcast live on BBC Radio and Television: BBC Radio 2 broadcasts from London's Hyde Park; and BBC Radio Ulster, BBC Radio Scotland and BBC Radio Wales broadcast their national events from Belfast, Glasgow and Swansea. Highlights of all four Proms in the Park events will be included as part of the live coverage of the Last Night of the Proms on BBC One and BBC Two, while digital TV viewers can choose via the red button between watching the concert inside the Royal Albert Hall and the various Proms in the Park events taking place across the country.

ns&i
Event sponsors

Note that all BBC Proms in the Park events take place outdoors and tickets are unreserved. The use of chairs is discouraged since it obstructs the view of others, but if you find it necessary because of limited mobility, please be considerate to your neighbours. In the interests of safety, please do not bring glass items, barbeques or flaming torches.

SATURDAY 13 SEPTEMBER

José Carreras *tenor*
Lesley Garrett *soprano*
Terry Wogan *presenter*

BBC Concert Orchestra
Martin Yates *conductor*

THE
ROYAL PARKS

José Carreras

This year the Last Night celebrations in Hyde Park include the grand finale of BBC Two's series *Maestro*. Join Terry Wogan and a host of international stars, including José Carreras, accompanied by Proms in the Park favourites the BBC Concert Orchestra, conducted by Martin Yates. The party gets under way with Abba tribute band Björn Again and all-male vocal group Teatro.

Gates open 4.00pm
Entertainment on stage from 5.30pm
For corporate hospitality facilities, call Charles Webb on 01484 437422, or visit sellershospitality.com

Tickets: £25.00 (under-3s free); Family and Friends ticket offer: buy 7 tickets and get the 8th ticket free. Tickets now available by phone from SEE TICKETS on 0844 412 4630* or online at bbc.co.uk/proms. Tickets available by post between 21 April and 19 May, using the Advance Booking Form (facing page 140); from 27 May tickets are also available at the Royal Albert Hall on 0845 401 5040* (9.00am–9.00pm). A £2.75 transaction fee applies to tickets purchased through the Royal Albert Hall; a £2.00 transaction fee applies to tickets purchased through SEE TICKETS. *Calls from a BT landline are charged at local rate; charges from mobiles and other networks may be higher.

Broadcast
RADIO Live on BBC Radio 2
ONLINE Live and 'listen again' options at bbc.co.uk/proms
TV Live via the red button on BBC Television

Tim Anderson (Proms in the Park)

SATURDAY 13 SEPTEMBER

Noel Thompson *presenter*

Ulster Orchestra
Kenneth Montgomery *conductor*

Noel Thompson presents the Ulster Orchestra under Principal Conductor Kenneth Montgomery and a host of local and international talent for Northern Ireland's classical music event of the year. The concert will be broadcast live on BBC Radio Ulster

Venue to be announced – see bbc.co.uk/proms for details. For ticket and other information, call the BBC NI Ticket Line on 0870 9011227†, minicom 0141 307 5701, or visit bbc.co.uk/ni/tickets. †Calls from a BT landline are charged at up to 8p per minute; charges from mobiles and other networks may be higher.

Noel Thompson

Kenneth Montgomery

Broadcast
RADIO Live on BBC Radio Ulster
ONLINE Live and 'listen again' options at bbc.co.uk/proms
TV Live via the red button on BBC Television

SATURDAY 13 SEPTEMBER

National Youth Choir of Scotland

BBC Scottish Symphony Orchestra
Robert Ziegler *conductor*

Join the BBC Scottish Symphony Orchestra for an unforgettable and spectacular evening, as we celebrate the Last Night of the Proms in true Scottish Style.

Tickets are free and available from the BBC Information Line on 08700 100 160†. Also available online at bbc.co.uk/proms. †Calls from a BT landline are charged at up to 8p per minute; charges from mobiles and other networks may be higher.

Robert Ziegler

Glasgow Green

Broadcast
RADIO Live on BBC Radio Scotland
ONLINE Live and 'listen again' options at bbc.co.uk/proms
TV Live via the red button on BBC Television

SATURDAY 13 SEPTEMBER

Gethin Jones *presenter*

Rebecca Evans *soprano*
Alfie Boe *tenor*

BBC National Chorus of Wales
BBC National Orchestra of Wales
David Charles Abell *conductor*

Singleton Park becomes the Bay of Naples for a night as the sixth BBC Proms in the Park from Swansea celebrates an evening of Italian music and Neapolitan song.

The BBC National Orchestra and Chorus of Wales, under conductor David Charles Abell, bring a festival of music to the city and link up with the Royal Albert Hall and Parks across the UK for the traditional Last Night celebrations. A Community Stage will host pre-concert performances and audience-participation singing, and fireworks will bring the evening to a climactic end.

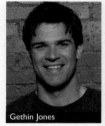
Gethin Jones

Tickets: £8.00 in advance, £10.00 on the day (under-12s free with accompanying adult). Available from the BBC National Orchestra of Wales Audience Line on 08700 131812†, open Monday–Friday 9.00am–9.00pm, Saturday 9.00am–5.00pm. Tickets are also available in person or by phone from the Grand Theatre, Singleton Street, Swansea (01792 475715†). Lines are open Monday–Sunday 9.30am–8.00pm, 9.30am–6.00pm on non-performance days. Also available online at bbc.co.uk/proms. †Calls from a BT landline are charged at up to 8p per minute; charges from mobiles and other networks may be higher.

Broadcast
RADIO Live on BBC Radio Wales
ONLINE Live and 'listen again' options at bbc.co.uk/proms
TV Live via the red button on BBC Television

HOW TO BOOK

ADVANCE BOOKING
By post and online
Monday 21 April – Monday 19 May

Use the Advance Booking Form or visit bbc.co.uk/proms

To take advantage of the Advance Booking period – and enjoy your best chance of securing the seats you want – you must use the Advance Booking Form (facing page 140) or the online ticket request system on the Proms website.

All postal and online bookings received before Monday 21 April will be treated as if they had arrived on that date and Express Bookings will then be handled first (for full details see page 139). Any bookings received after Monday 19 May will be treated as general bookings, and dealt with from Tuesday 27 May.

Please note that bookings can not be accepted by fax.

Postal address: BBC Proms, Box Office, Royal Albert Hall, London SW7 2AP
Online booking: bbc.co.uk/proms

For Concert Listings, see pages 92–129

GENERAL BOOKING
In person, by phone or online – opens Tuesday 27 May

In person: The Royal Albert Hall Box Office is located at Door 12 and is open 9.00am–9.00pm daily. Note that no booking fee applies to tickets bought in person at the Hall.

Telephone: 0845 401 5040 *Calls from a BT landline are charged at local rate. Charges from mobiles or other networks may be higher.*
Online booking: bbc.co.uk/proms

THE LAST NIGHT OF THE PROMS

Because of the high demand for tickets for the Last Night of the Proms, special booking arrangements apply. For full details – and your chance to enter the Last Night Ballot – see page 137.

PROMMING ON THE DAY – Don't book, just turn up

Up to 1,400 standing places are available for each concert at the Royal Albert Hall. Over 500 Arena and Gallery tickets are always on sale at the door from an hour beforehand, so you can just turn up on the day. Additionally, Weekend Promming Passes and Season Tickets can be booked in advance: see pages 136 and 139.

PROMS CHAMBER MUSIC AT CADOGAN HALL

For booking information for concerts at Cadogan Hall, see page 132.

PROMS PLUS AT THE ROYAL COLLEGE OF MUSIC

Proms Plus, the series of free pre- and post-concert events, takes place in the Britten Theatre at the Royal College of Music, opposite the south side of the Royal Albert Hall. For more information, see pages 70–72, page 133, and the listings section from page 92.

The Royal Albert Hall

ROYAL ALBERT HALL

Leith's are the official caterers at the Royal Albert Hall providing a wide range of food and drink within the bars, restaurants and boxes.

Restaurants

Café Consort is fully licensed and offers a menu of contemporary dishes. Post-concert drinks and light meals are also available on selected dates.

Recently refurbished, **Coda** is a new restaurant offering an elegant dining experience with a modern British menu.

The **Elgar Restaurant** offers a varied menu catering for all tastes with views over Hyde Park.

The **Lanson Arena Bar** serves a selection of light dishes.

The restaurants open two hours before the performance, except the Café Consort which opens two-and-a-half hours before. Tables should be booked in advance, except for the Lanson Arena Bar. Call the Box Office on 0845 401 5040* to make your reservation.

Bars

Bars are located on all but the Gallery level, offering a full range of drinks, sandwiches, confectionery and ice cream. The Lanson Arena Bar, North Circle Bar and Champagne Bar open two hours prior to each concert. All other bars open 45 minutes before the start of the performance.

Interval orders

Interval orders can be arranged from any bar. Please ask any member of bar staff.

Box hospitality

If you have seats in one of the Hall's boxes, you can pre-order catering. Please call 020 7589 5666 for details. Orders should then be placed in writing at least two working days before the concert that you attending.

Please note Leith's do not permit the consumption of your own food and drink in the Hall, with the exception of cold soft drinks in closed plastic containers. In the interests of health and safety, glasses and bottles are not allowed in the auditorium, except as part of box hospitality ordered through Leith's.

Car Parking A limited number of parking spaces, priced £7.50 each, is available from 6.00pm (or one hour before weekend matinee concerts)

Coda: an elegant dining experience in the Royal Albert Hall's newest restaurant

in the Imperial College car park (Prince Consort or Exhibition Road entrances). These can be booked using the Advance Booking Form (facing page 140), online (from 21 April) or by calling the Box Office on 0845 401 5040*, 9.00am–9.00pm daily (from 27 May). Please note that if attending both early-evening and late-night concerts only one parking fee is payable.

Doors open 45 minutes before the start of each concert (earlier for restaurant and bar access).

Latecomers will not be admitted into the auditorium unless or until there is a suitable break in the music. There is a screen in the Door 6 foyer with a digital audio relay.

Bags and coats may be left in the cloakrooms at Door 9 (ground level) and at basement level beneath Door 6. For reasons of safety and comfort only small bags are permitted in the Arena.

Security In the interests of safety, bags may be searched upon entry.

Children under 5 Out of consideration for both audience and artists, children under the age of 5 are not allowed in the auditorium.

Dress code Come as you are: there is no dress code at the Proms.

Mobile phones and watch alarms should be turned off.

The use of cameras, video cameras and recording equipment is strictly forbidden.

Smoking is not permitted at the Royal Albert Hall.

Tours of the Royal Albert Hall

Tours run every day, except Wednesday, and last approximately one hour. To book and to check availability, please call 020 7838 3105. Ticket prices range from £5.00 to £8.00 per person, with a number of concessions available.

Royal Albert Hall Shop

The Royal Albert Hall Shop, offering a selection of Proms and Royal Albert Hall gifts and souvenirs, is located in the South Porch at Door 12. The Shop is open daily from 10.00am to 6.00pm. Proms merchandise can also be purchased at the Door 6 foyer during performance times.

Cadogan Hall

Cadogan Hall

5 Sloane Terrace, London SW1X 9DQ *(see map, page 134)*

www.cadoganhall.com

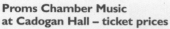

The Proms Chamber Music series – now in its 13th year – returns to Cadogan Hall in the heart of Chelsea. The more intimate setting in one of London's newest concert halls promises to bring a different perspective to many of this year's anniversary composers. There's Vaughan Williams from Mark Padmore and the Nash Ensemble, and Messiaen from Gweneth-Ann Jeffers and Pierre-Laurent Aimard, who will also bring music by Elliott Carter. Julia Fischer and Yakov Kreizberg (who will also be appearing together at the Royal Albert Hall this season) bring a programme of Grieg and Tchaikovsky. There's music from earlier ages from Jordi Savall, Christophe Rousset and I Fagiolini, and the series ends with a varied programme from Radio 3 New Generation Artists Elizabeth Watts and the Aronowitz Ensemble, including the world premiere of a new commission by Huw Watkins.

Detailed concert listings can be found from page 92.

Proms Chamber Music (PCM) concerts are broadcast live on BBC Radio 3 and are repeated the following Saturday at 2.00 pm

Doors open at 12 noon; entrance to the auditorium will be from half an hour before start-time

Proms Chamber Music at Cadogan Hall – ticket prices

Stalls: £10.00; Centre Gallery: £8.00
Day seats (Side Gallery): £5.00

Advance Booking, 21 April–19 May
To book tickets during the Advance Booking period, use the Booking Form (facing page 140) or the online ticket request system (at bbc.co.uk/proms).

General Booking, from Tuesday 27 May
Once General Booking has opened, you can also book tickets by telephone or in person at Cadogan Hall (on 020 7730 4500) or at the Royal Albert Hall (on 0845 401 5040*), as well as online.

Tickets can be bought on the day of the concert – from Cadogan Hall only – from 10.00am.

£5.00 tickets on the day
At least 150 Side Gallery (bench) seats will be available for just £5.00 each from 10.00am on the day of the concert. These tickets can only be bought at Cadogan Hall. They must be purchased in person and with cash only, and are limited to two tickets per transaction.

£30.00 PCM Series Pass
Hear all eight PCM concerts for just £30.00, with guaranteed entrance to the Side Gallery until 12.50pm (after which PCM Series Pass-holders may be asked to join the day queue).

During the Advance Booking period (Monday 21 April – Monday 19 May), PCM Series Passes can be purchased using the Advance Booking Form (facing page 140) or the online ticket request system (at bbc.co.uk/proms). Two passport-sized photographs must be provided.

Once General Booking has opened (on Tuesday 27 May), PCM Series Passes can also be purchased by telephone or in person at the Royal Albert Hall (on 0845 401 5040*) as well as online.

Note that PCM Series Passes cannot be purchased from Cadogan Hall.

PCM Series Passes are subject to availability.

Royal College of Music, Britten Theatre

Royal College of Music, Britten Theatre
Prince Consort Road,
London SW7 2BS *(see map, page 134)*

www.rcm.ac.uk

Proms Plus – the newly extended series of free pre- and post-concert events complementing the main Proms concerts at the Royal Albert Hall – takes place in the Royal College of Music's Britten Theatre. Along with familiar events such as Composer Portraits and Music Intros, this year sees the first ever Proms Literary Festival and a live edition of Radio 3's *In Tune* on the First Night, featuring special guests and live music.

For more details about the Proms Plus series, including ticket information, see pages 70–72; for specific event details see the daily listings from page 92.

Getting there

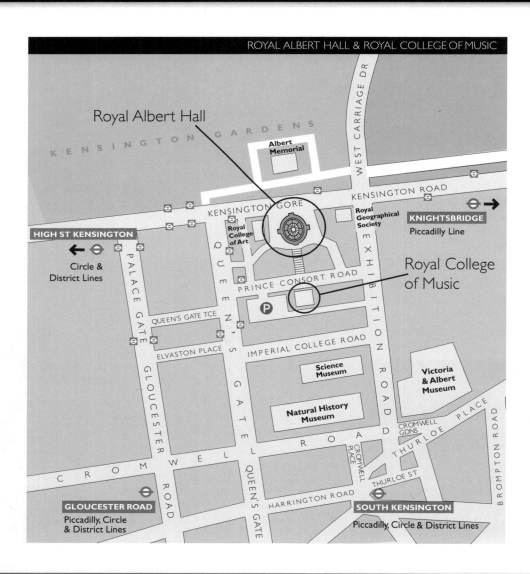

ROYAL ALBERT HALL & ROYAL COLLEGE OF MUSIC

Royal Albert Hall

Royal College of Music

The following buses serve the Royal Albert Hall and Royal College of Music (via Kensington Gore, Queen's Gate, Palace Gate and/or Prince Consort Road): 9/N9, 10/N10, 49, 52/N52, 70, 74, 360 & 452.

The following buses serve Cadogan Hall (via Sloane Street and/or Sloane Square): 11, 19, 22, 137, 211, 319, 360, 452 & C1..

For 24-hour London travel information, call 020 7222 1234 or visit www.tfl.gov.uk.

There are bicycle racks near Door 11 of the Royal Albert Hall. (Neither the Hall nor the BBC can accept responsibility for items lost or stolen from these racks.) The Royal Albert Hall is unable to accept folding bicycles in the cloakrooms.

Please note All Proms venues lie inside the Congestion Charging Zone which operates 7.00am–6.00pm Mon–Fri.

For car parking at the Royal Albert Hall, see page 131.

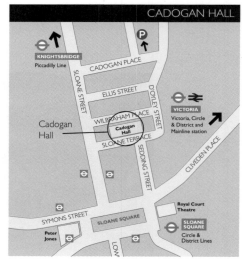

CADOGAN HALL

Cadogan Hall

Access at the Proms

Royal Albert Hall
Please call the Access Information Line on 020 7838 3110 for advice on facilities for disabled concert-goers (including car parking) at the Royal Albert Hall; if you have any special requirements; or to request a Royal Albert Hall Access Guide. Dedicated staff will be available daily from 9.00am to 9.00pm. The Access Guide is also available at www.royalalberthall.com.

The Royal Albert Hall has up to 20 spaces bookable for wheelchair-users and their companions (entrance via Door 8). There are two end-of-aisle places in the Side Stalls, and two in the Centre Stalls – these places are priced as such; front-row platform places either side of the stage are priced as Side Stalls seats; rear platform places are priced as Front Circle seats. Spaces in the Front Circle are priced as such. When filling in the Booking Form, tick your preferred price range (*ie* Centre Stalls, Side Stalls or Front Circle) and enter the number of places required under the 'Wheelchair space' column.

Four wheelchair spaces are available in the Gallery for Promming. These cannot be pre-booked. (See page 57, 'Promming at a glance'.)

Passenger lifts at the Royal Albert Hall are located on the ground-floor corridor at Doors 1 and 8. Use of lifts is discouraged during performances.

Cadogan Hall
Cadogan Hall has a range of services to assist disabled customers, including provision for wheelchair-users in the Stalls. There are three wheelchair spaces available for advance booking and one space reserved for sale from 10.00am on the day of the concert. For information, call 020 7730 4500.

Royal College of Music
The Royal College of Music has two spaces for wheelchair-users in its theatre. Direct access is available through the Imperial College campus by arrangement. Where possible, 48 hours' notice is appreciated. Please call 020 7589 3643.

Discounts for disabled concert-goers
Disabled concert-goers (and one companion) receive a 50% discount on all ticket prices (except Arena and Gallery areas) for concerts at the Royal Albert Hall and Cadogan Hall. To claim this discount, tick the box on the Advance Booking Form, or call the Access Information Line on 020 7838 3110 (from Tuesday 27 May) if booking by phone. Note that discounts for disabled concert-goers cannot be combined with other ticket offers.

The BBC Proms: access for all

Tickets can also be purchased in person from Tuesday 27 May at the Royal Albert Hall. The Box Office is situated at Door 12 and has ramped access, an induction loop and drop-down counters.

Hard-of-hearing and visually impaired concert-goers
The Royal Albert Hall has an infra-red system with a number of personal receivers for use with and without hearing aids. To make use of the service, collect a free receiver from the Door 6 Information Desk.

If you have a guide dog, the best place to sit in the Royal Albert Hall is in a Loggia or Second Tier Box, where your dog may stay with you. If you are sitting elsewhere, stewards will be happy to look after your dog while you enjoy the concert. Please call the Access Information Line on 020 7838 3110 in advance of your visit to organise.

Proms Guide: non-print versions
Audio CD, Braille and CD-R versions of this Guide are available in two parts, 'Articles' and 'Concert Listings/Booking Information', priced £3.00 each or £6.00 for both. For more information and to order, call RNIB Customer Services on 0845 7023 153 (calls from a BT landline are charged at local rate).

Advance Booking
Assistance is available for visually impaired patrons wishing to make Advance Booking requests. Please call the Access Information Line on 020 7838 3110.

Radio 3 commentary
Visually impaired patrons are welcome to use the free infra-red hearing facility (*see above*) to listen in to the broadcast commentary on Radio 3.

Programme-reading service
Ask at the Door 6 Information Desk if you would like a steward to read your concert programme out to you.

Large-print programmes & texts
Large-print concert programmes can be made available on the night (at the same price as the standard programme) if ordered not less than five working days in advance. Complimentary large-print texts and opera librettos (where applicable) can also be made available on the night if ordered in advance. To order any large-print programmes or texts, please call 020 7765 3260. They will be left for collection at the Door 6 Information Desk 45 minutes before the start of the concert.

Special Offers

SAME-DAY SAVER

Same-Day Savers

If you book for more than one concert on the same day, you are entitled to save £4.00 per ticket for each subsequent concert.

This offer applies to matinee, evening and late-night performances in the Royal Albert Hall only. It is not valid for Arena, Gallery and Circle (Restricted View) price areas, or for concerts at Cadogan Hall.

Kids go half-price

The Proms are a great way to discover live music, and we encourage anyone over 5 years old to attend. Tickets for under-16s can be purchased at half-price in any seating area for all Proms except the Last Night (Prom 76).

Note that the Doctor Who Prom (Prom 13) is expressly designed to introduce young children to concert-going.

Great Savings for Groups

Groups of 10 or more can claim a 10% discount (5% for C band concerts) on the price of Centre/Side Stalls or Front/Rear Circle tickets (excluding the Last Night).

For more information, call the Group Booking Information Line on 020 7838 3108.

Please note that group purchases cannot be made online during the General Booking period.

Proms in the Park Friends and Family Group Ticket

Make a real party of the Last Night in Hyde Park – buy 7 tickets and get the 8th ticket free.

The BBC Proms: a great way to discover live music

WEEKEND PROMMING PASS

Beat the queues at the weekend and save money! Promming is an essential part of the character of the BBC Proms (see pages 52–57). In addition to discounted tickets, the Weekend Promming Pass offers guaranteed access up to 10 minutes before start-time to the Arena or Gallery standing areas for all concerts in the Royal Albert Hall on Fridays, Saturdays and Sundays (excluding Proms 13, 75 and 76). Passes can be purchased in advance, by post (using the Advance Booking Form) or online, and – from Tuesday 27 May – by phone or in person at the Box Office. Passes are available up to 6.00pm on the day they start (NB 6.30pm on 18 July & 1 August, 5.30pm on 8 & 22 August). Prices vary for each weekend depending on the number of concerts covered.

Note that Weekend 2 excludes the Doctor Who Prom (Prom 13); Weekend 6 includes Bank Holiday Monday (25 August); and there is no pass covering Proms 75 and 76. Passes are not valid for concerts at Cadogan Hall.

Passes are non-transferable and signature ID may be requested upon entry. Purchase of a Weekend Promming Pass does not guarantee entry to the Last Night, but tickets may be counted towards the 'Six-Concert Rule' (see opposite) in conjunction with further Passes or Day Ticket stubs.

Note that you may purchase a maximum of four passes per weekend (subject to availability). For Whole and Half-Season Tickets, see page 139.

Weekend Promming Pass prices		
Weekend 1	Proms 1–5	£17.50
Weekend 2	Proms 11, 12 & 14	£12.50
Weekend 3	Proms 19–23	£22.50
Weekend 4	Proms 29–33	£22.50
Weekend 5	Proms 40–43	£17.50
Weekend 6	Proms 48–52	£22.50
Weekend 7	Proms 58–61	£17.50
Weekend 8	Proms 68–70	£12.50

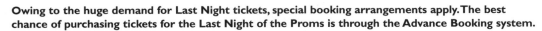

The Last Night

Owing to the huge demand for Last Night tickets, special booking arrangements apply. The best chance of purchasing tickets for the Last Night of the Proms is through the Advance Booking system.

Advance Booking for the Last Night

The Six-Concert Rule

In order to apply for any tickets for the Last Night during the Advance Booking period (21 April – 19 May), you must book for at least six other concerts at the Royal Albert Hall in the 2008 season. (*Please note that Prom 4 and concerts at Cadogan Hall do not count towards the Six-Concert Rule.*)

Book one ticket in the same seating area for at least six other concerts and you can apply at the same time for a single ticket in the same seating area for the Last Night. For example, book one ticket in the Choir for six concerts, and you can apply for one ticket in the Choir for the Last Night.

Book two *or more* tickets in the same seating area for at least six other concerts in the 2008 season and you can apply at the same time for a maximum of *two* tickets in the same seating area for the Last Night (*ie* whether you book two or 22 Stalls tickets for six concerts, you can still apply for only two Stalls tickets for the Last Night).

Note that if you book tickets for at least six other concerts but in different seating areas, you will be allocated Last Night seats in the area of the majority of your bookings (unless you specify that lower-priced tickets are desired).

We regret that, if the Last Night is sold out by the time your application is processed, no refunds for other tickets purchased will be payable.

General Booking for the Last Night

Once General Booking opens (on Tuesday 27 May), the Six-Concert Rule no longer applies. Last Night tickets have usually sold out by this stage, but returns occasionally become available for sale, so it is always worth checking with the Box Office.

Please note that for all Last Night bookings, only one application (for a maximum of two tickets) can be made per household.

Promming at the Last Night

Day Prommers and Weekend Promming Pass holders who have attended six or more other concerts (in either the Arena or the Gallery) can buy one ticket each for the Last Night (priced £5.00) on presentation of their used tickets at the Box Office on or after Tuesday 22 July (subject to availability).

Season Ticket-holders Whole Season Tickets include admission to the Last Night. A limited allocation of Last Night places is also reserved for Half-Season Ticket-holders. Holders of First Half Season Tickets can buy one ticket each (priced £5.00) at the Box Office from Wednesday 23 July (subject to availability). Holders of Second Half Season Tickets can buy tickets in the same way from Wednesday 20 August (subject to availability).

Queuing Whole Season Ticket-holders and other Prommers with Last Night tickets are guaranteed entrance until 10 minutes before the concert. All Prommers (Day or Season) with Last Night tickets should queue on the South Steps, west side (Arena) or the top of Bremner Road, left side (Gallery).

Sleeping Out There has long been a tradition of Prommers with Last Night tickets sleeping out overnight to secure their preferred standing place inside the Hall. The official queues will form at 4.00pm on the last Friday of the season. Those also wishing to attend Prom 75 will be given numbered slips to reserve their places in the queue, but must return in person immediately after the end of the concert.

On the Night Standing tickets are usually still available on the Last Night itself (priced £5.00, one per person). No previous ticket purchases are necessary. Just join the queue on the South Steps, east side (Arena) or the top of Bremner Road, right side (Gallery) during the afternoon and you may well be lucky.

Last Night Ballot

One hundred Centre Stalls seats (priced £82.50 each) for the Last Night of the Proms at the Royal Albert Hall will be allocated by ballot. The 'Six-Concert Rule' does not apply, and no other ticket purchases are necessary. Only one application (for a maximum of two tickets) may be made per household.

If you would like to apply for tickets by ballot, please complete the official Ballot Form on the back of this slip (photocopies are not acceptable) and send it by post only – to arrive no later than Thursday 10 July – to:

BBC Proms Ballot,
Box Office,
Royal Albert Hall,
London SW7 2AP

Note that the Proms Ballot application is completely separate from other Proms booking procedures. Envelopes should be clearly addressed to 'BBC Proms Ballot' and should contain only the official Ballot Form, together with your cheque or credit/debit card details. If sending a cheque, please also enclose an SAE so that it can be returned to you if your application is unsuccessful. Successful applicants will be notified by post within two weeks of the ballot, which takes place on Friday 11 July.

This form is also available to download from bbc.co.uk/proms; or call 020 7765 5407 to receive a copy of this form by post.

The personal information given on this form will not be used for any purpose by the BBC or the Royal Albert Hall other than this ballot.

Last Night Ballot

Title _____ Initial _____

Surname _____

Address _____

_____

_____

Postcode _____

Country _____

Daytime tel. _____

Please tick the appropriate boxes

☐ I wish to apply for one ticket (£82.50)

☐ I wish to apply for two tickets (£165.00)

☐ I enclose a cheque made payable to 'Royal Albert Hall' and an SAE. (Cheques will be returned to unsuccessful applicants within two weeks of the ballot.)

☐ Please debit my Visa/Amex/Mastercard/Solo/Electron/Maestro card

☐☐☐☐☐☐☐☐☐☐☐☐☐☐☐☐☐☐☐

Start date ☐☐ / ☐☐   Issue no. ☐☐

Expiry date ☐☐ / ☐☐   Maestro only

Security code (CVV no.) ☐☐☐☐

last 3 digits on back of card (Visa/Mastercard); 4 digits on front (Amex)

Signature _____

Choose Your Seat

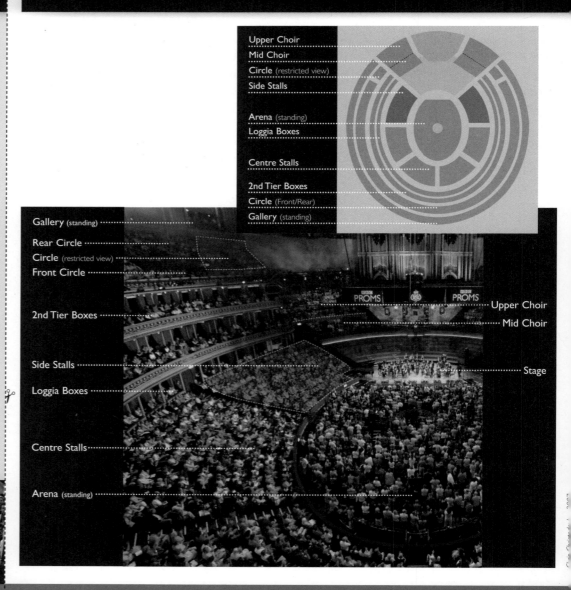

Upper Choir
Mid Choir
Circle (restricted view)
Side Stalls
Arena (standing)
Loggia Boxes
Centre Stalls
2nd Tier Boxes
Circle (Front/Rear)
Gallery (standing)

Gallery (standing)
Rear Circle
Circle (restricted view)
Front Circle
2nd Tier Boxes
Side Stalls
Loggia Boxes
Centre Stalls
Arena (standing)

Upper Choir
Mid Choir
Stage

Ticket Prices

Seats

Concerts fall into one of seven different price bands – indicated above each concert listing on pages 92–127.

	A	B	C	D	E	F	G
Centre Stalls	£26.00	£36.00	£44.00	£15.00	£17.50	£82.50	
Side Stalls	£24.00	£32.00	£40.00	£15.00	£17.50	£80.00	
Grand Tier Boxes	£35.00	£44.00	£54.00	£15.00	£17.50	£90.00	
12 seats, price per seat	(As many Grand Tier Boxes are privately owned, availability is limited)						
Loggia Boxes 8 seats, price per seat	£30.00	£40.00	£48.00	£15.00	£17.50	£85.00	
2nd Tier Boxes 5 seats, price per seat	£20.00	£25.00	£35.00	£15.00	£17.50	£72.50	
Mid Choir	£18.00	£21.00	£30.00	N/A	£17.50	£60.00	
Upper Choir	£16.00	£19.00	£26.00	N/A	£12.50	£55.00	
Front Circle	£13.00	£16.00	£20.00	£10.00	£12.50	£55.00	
Rear Circle	£10.00	£11.00	£15.00	£10.00	£12.50	£40.00	
Circle (restricted view)	£6.00	£7.00	£10.00	N/A	£8.00	£20.00	

G: ALL SEATS £10.00 (UNDER-16s £5.00)

Promming (standing)

Standing places are available in the Arena and Gallery on the day for £5.00 (see pages 52–57)

Season Tickets	Dates	Arena	Gallery
Whole Season (Proms 1–76)	18 July – 13 September	£190.00	£170.00
Half Season tickets			
First Half (Proms 1–39)	18 July – 14 August	£110.00	£95.00
Second Half (Proms 40–75)	15 August – 13 September	£110.00	£95.00

Please note that booking fees apply to all postal, telephone and online bookings (for details, see Booking Form).
Unwanted tickets may be exchanged for tickets to other Proms concerts (subject to availability). A fee of £1.00 per ticket will be charged for this service. Telephone the Royal Albert Hall Box Office (0845 401 5040*) for further details.

BBC Proms in the Park, Hyde Park, London, Saturday 13 September

All tickets £25.00 (for further details of this and other Proms in the Park venues, see pages 128–129)
Friends and Family Group Ticket: buy 7 tickets and get the 8th ticket free.

Express Bookings

All booking forms that include a request for an A band concert qualify for Express Booking. To increase your chances of getting the tickets you want for the more popular concerts in price bands B and C, you are advised to book for at least one A band concert as well.
NB: If you are only booking for the Doctor Who Prom (price band G), your booking will also qualify for fast-tracking. Tick the box at the end of the Advance Booking Form if you think your application qualifies.

Disabled concert-goers

See page 135 for details of special discounts, access and facilities.

Privately owned seats

A high proportion of boxes, as well as 650 Stalls seats, are privately owned. Unless returned by owners, these seats are not usually available for sale.

Season Tickets

Season Tickets and PCM Series Passes can be booked by post or online from Monday 21 April and by phone or in person at the Royal Albert Hall Box Office from Tuesday 27 May. For postal bookings, complete the special section of the Booking Form (facing page 140). Please note that two passport-sized photographs must be provided for each ticket or pass before it can be issued.

Proms at Cadogan Hall

For booking information on the Proms Chamber Music series, see page 132.

How to fill in the Booking Form

- **Choose the concerts** you want to go to and where you want to sit.
- **Enter the number of tickets** you require for each concert under your chosen seating area (adult tickets on the white squares, under-16s on the blue).
- **Add up the value of tickets** requested referring to the price bands on page 139, and enter the amount in the 'Sub-total' column.
- **If claiming any special offers** (see page 136) or disabled concert-goers' discounts (see page 135), enter the total value of discounts claimed for each concert in the red 'Discount' column. Then subtract the value of the discount from the 'Sub-total' and enter the 'Total' at the end of the row (adding in any car parking fee, if applicable).

- **If the tickets you request are not available**, you can opt to receive lower- or higher-priced alternatives by ticking the appropriate box at the end of the Booking Form. Ticking one or both of these boxes increases your chances of securing tickets for the most popular concerts.

Booking Queries
If you have any queries about how to fill in the Booking Form, call the Box Office on 0845 401 5040* open 9.00am–9.00pm daily. *Calls from a BT landline are charged at local rate. Charges from mobiles or other networks may be higher.

Online Booking
For details of how to book online, visit bbc.co.uk/proms Note that once General Booking opens (on Tuesday 27 May), online customers will be able to choose their own seats.

Check List
Before posting your booking form, please check that you have:
- [ ] Filled in your name at the top of both sides.
- [ ] Indicated whether you will accept lower- or higher-priced tickets.
- [ ] Entered your data protection preferences.
- [ ] Enclosed two passport-sized photographs for each Proms Season Ticket or PCM Series Pass applied for.

ADVANCE BOOKING FORM PART 1 — Full name of sender: Surname *Penny*, First Name *Tim*

ADVANCE BOOKING FORM PART 2 — Full name of sender: Surname *Penny*, First Name *Tim*

Part 1 – Sub-total £ 863·50

Prommers' Season Tickets See page 133

		Arena	Gallery
Whole Season	Proms 1–76 (Friday 18 July–Saturday 13 September)	£190	£170
First Half	Proms 1–39 (Friday 18 July–Thursday 14 August)	£110	£95
Second Half	Proms 40–75 (Friday 15 August–Friday 12 September)	£110	£95

Weekend Promming Pass See page 136 Note that you can book a maximum of four passes per weekend

BBC Proms at Cadogan Hall See page 132

BBC Proms in the Park, Hyde Park, London, Saturday 13 September

	Number of tickets	Sub-total	Discount (see page 136)	Sub-total	Total (£)
All tickets: £25.00	8	£ 200·00	25·00		175·00

Friends and Family: Buy 7 tickets and get the 8th ticket free

Part 2 – sum of Sub-totals £ 175·00

Part 1 total	Part 2 total	Booking fee	Grand Total
Sum of totals £ 863·50	+ £ 175·00	+ £2.75 =	£ 1041·25

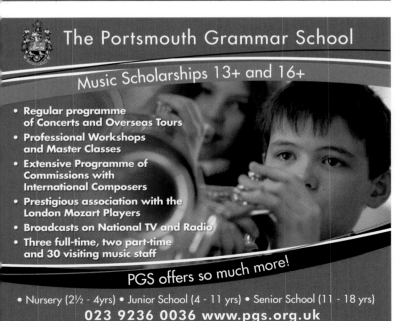
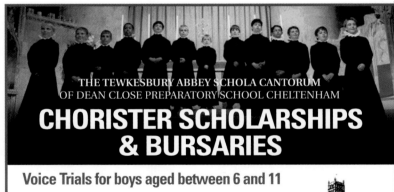

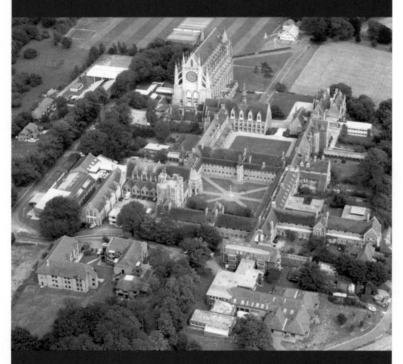

Come and sing on a bigger stage!

The BBC Symphony Chorus

The BBC Symphony Chorus is one of the finest and most distinctive amateur choirs in the UK. In its appearances with the BBC Symphony Orchestra, the Chorus undertakes a wide range of challenging repertoire which is usually broadcast on BBC Radio 3. This season's concerts with the BBC SO have included John Foulds's *A World Requiem* in the Royal Albert Hall, Penderecki's Symphony No. 8, and music by Vaughan Williams, Holst and Ives conducted by Sir Andrew Davis, the Chorus's President. The Chorus has recently performed in the Canary Islands, Brussels and Istanbul and makes regular recordings.

As resident chorus for the BBC Proms, the Chorus gives five or six concerts each season, including the Last Night, and often a 'solo' Prom of its own under its Director, Stephen Jackson. This year's performances include Verdi's *Requiem* and Janáček's *Glagolitic Mass* with the BBC SO, conducted by Jiří Bělohlávek and Pierre Boulez respectively, plus Finzi's *Intimations of Immortality* with the BBC Concert Orchestra and Messiaen's *La Transfiguration* with the BBC National Orchestra and Chorus of Wales.

Would you like to join us?

Do you love singing? Do you want to make music at the highest level with great conductors and orchestras? Would you like to work on new and challenging repertoire, as well as standard choral works, with a dynamic chorus director and lively, sociable singers? If the answer is 'yes', then the BBC Symphony Chorus is the choir for you! Membership is free and includes individual vocal training. New members are always welcome.

To find out more, visit bbc.co.uk/symphonychorus or contact Lydia Casey, Administrator, BBC Symphony Chorus, BBC Maida Vale Studios, Delaware Road, London W9 2LG
Email: lydia.casey@bbc.co.uk Tel: 020 7765 4715

2008-09 Season Highlights

As part of the BBC Symphony Orchestra's 2008-09 Barbican season, the BBC Symphony Chorus will perform:

Beethoven *Missa solemnis* • **Orff** *Carmina burana* • **Poulenc** *Stabat Mater* • **Ravel** *Daphnis and Chloë, Suite No. 2* • **Bruckner** *Mass No. 3 in F minor*

Plus **Messiaen** *La Transfiguration* with the Philharmonia Orchestra and an *a cappella* concert featuring **Poulenc** *Figure humaine*.

INDEX OF ARTISTS

Bold italic figures refer to Prom numbers
(**PCM** indicates Proms Chamber Music concerts, Mondays at 1.00pm)
* first appearance at a BBC Henry Wood Promenade Concert
† current/‡former member of BBC Radio 3's New Generation Artists scheme

INDEX OF WORKS

Bold italic figures refer to Prom numbers
(**PCM** indicates Proms Chamber Music concerts, Mondays at 1.00pm)
* first performance at a BBC Henry Wood Promenade Concert

BBC Proms 2008
Director Roger Wright, Controller BBC Radio 3 and Director
BBC Proms
Personal Assistant Yvette Pusey

Artistic Administrator Rosemary Gent
Concerts Administrator Helen Heslop
Concerts Assistants Tamsin Bainbridge, Alys Jones
TV Concerts Assistant Holly Traynor

Marketing Manager Kate Finch
Publicists Victoria Bevan, Rebecca Driver
Publicity Assistant Carly Coughlan
Marketing Co-ordinator Catherine Chew
Learning and Audience Development Co-ordinator Ellara Wakely

Management Assistant Tricia Twigg

Editor, BBC Radio 3 Edward Blakeman
Editor, TV Classical Music Oliver Macfarlane
Project Manager, Proms in the Park Ian Russell

BBC Proms 2008 Guide
Editor Edward Bhesania
Design Premm Design Ltd, London
Cover illustration © Andy Potts
Concert introductions written by James Jolly

Publications Editor John Bryant
Publications Designer Tania Conrad
Publications Officer Mary Galloway
Editorial Assistant Clara Nissen

Published by BBC Proms Publications,
Room 1045, Broadcasting House, London W1A 1AA

Distributed by Random House, 20 Vauxhall Bridge Road,
London SW1V 2SA

Advertising Cabbell Publishing Ltd, London (020 8971 8450)

Printed by Linney Print, Mansfield

 This publication has been designed to be recycled.
Please recycle it when you are finished

© BBC 2008   ISBN 978-1-84607-526-1